FAMILY PLANNING IN URBAN SLUM—

ITS ANALYSIS & IMPLICATIONS

Sumathy S. Rao

1991

DAYA PUBLISHING HOUSE

DELHI - 110 006

ISBN 81-7035-103-0

Published by: Anil Mittal for Daya Publishing House, at 1302, Vaid Wara, Nai Sarak, Delhi-110006. Phone: 260116.

Laser Typeset by Computer Codes, Delhi-110009. Phone : 7241200.
Printed at A.P. OFFSET, Delhi-110032.

PRINTED IN INDIA

ACKNOWLEDGEMENTS

I owe a deep sense of gratitude to my Research Supervisor Dr. K. Mahadevan, Professor, Department of Population Studies, Sri Venkateswara University, Tirupati for his valuable and encouraging guidance through the course of the study. I am very thankful to him for his meticulous care in putting me on the right track.

I am grateful to Dr. N. Audinarayana, Lecturer in Population Studies, Bharatiar University, Coimbatore, for his timely help and co-operation in completing my dissertation.

I am very thankful to Dr. R. Jayasree, Project Officer, Centre for Adult Education and Extension Studies, Bharatiar University, Coimbatore for her assistance during this study.

I am also thankful to Shri Despande, Computer Programmer of the IIPS, Bombay and Dr. S. Sivaraju for his valuable suggestions and assistance in computer analysis.

In addition a number of close associates helped me in different ways from time to time in completing this study. They include Dr. V. Kapali, WHO, Leprosy Consultant, Tamil Nadu; Mrs. Padmini Siva Subramanian, Chairman, Adult Literacy Community Welfare Committee, Women's Voluntary Services, Madras; Mr. Domenic Azuh, Research Scholar, Deptt. of Population Studies, S.V. University, Tirupati.

I am thankful to Mr. N. Lokanadhan, and Mr. D.V. Chalapathy for their excellent Secretarial Assistance.

Lastly my sincere thanks to the respondents of this study who had the patience and co-operation for the successful completion of this study.

TIRUPATI

SUMATHY S. RAO

FOREWORD

India is passing through a period of unprecedented population growth since 1940s. The birth and death rates almost equalled till 1921 since the population growth recorded between 1891 and 1921 was not more than 5%. As against this, the population grew by 77% between 1921-61. It has almost doubled during the three decades 1951-1981, with the 1981 census population being 685 million. While intensified governmental efforts at population control from 1960s have succeeded in reducing the acceleration in growth, current population growth rate still hovers around 2.1% per annum. The present population is about 840 million and about 48 babies are born every minute. According to current estimates, the population will, anyway, grow to 994 million by the year 2000.

This unprecedented growth in population is not restricted to India alone but continues to be a global phenomena. The world's population which stood at less than one billion in 1800 has risen to 2 billion by 1950, to 3.5 billion by 1969 and is expected to reach 6.3 billion by the year 2000. But an alarming feature of the growth is that 86% of the population growth between 1950 and 1980 and 84% between 1980 and 2000 has been and will be contributed by the developing nations. Of the expected 6.3 billion population in the year 2000, 5 billion will belong to the developing countries. Of this, the share of India and China will be 1.0 and 1.2 billion respectively.

Recognising the serious consequences of rapid population growth to economic and social development, most of the developing countries have, during the past 3-4 decades, mounted family planning programmes aimed at slowing the population growth. So far about 42 developing countries have adopted official policies to reduce population growth by fixing specific demographic targets and setting up institutional mechanisms to translate the policies into action. The most populous countries like China, India, Indonesia, Bangladesh and Pakistan are among these. The basic objective of most of these family planning programmes is to achieve a reduction in birth rate, primarily, by making available to the people effective family planning services and information. Simultaneously, however, there are evidences from worldwide multidisciplinary research that fertility control is a much more complex problem that envisaged, and that birth rates are affected not only by availability of family planning services, but also by social, economic and cultural conditions that determine how many children people want and how intensely they desire to limit their child bearing. The importance attached by the protagonists of the latter view is reflected in their assertion that 'Development is the best form of contraception'. A number of country studies and cross-country studies have, therefore, been carried out during the past 2-3 decades to measure the relative importance of Demand Vs Supply Interventions for fertility control. Such studies have yielded valuable information for policy and programme planners in the population field and are still continuing; the present study by the author should be viewed as part of these efforts.

While substantial knowledge has been generated, mostly at macro level, on variables that are crucial in influencing both the Demand and Supply side of the fertility control programme, there is further need to test their validity and applicability at the micro level and in various geographic and cultural settings. India is not lagging behind in these studies and we know much more today than what we knew ten years back on factors that need to be influenced to make the programmes yield better results. We know today that developing countries will not have to pass through the type of sequential economic and social development that the present day developed countries passed through in order to bring about a rapid decline in fertility; on the other hand a different type of development related to health, education and alleviation of poverty will be powerful enough to bring down fertility. Crucial among these are reduction in infant and child mortality, improving female education and status, reducing poverty, provision of effective and acceptable family planning services and a communication programme that cannot only transmit messages but can educate and influence couples, families and communities.

The present study by the author adds to the pool of knowledge already available. The study is significant in that it has been carried out in the slum areas of the major metropolitan city of Madras. Slum areas are considered difficult to approach physically, difficult to penetrate into the minds of the occupants; and have a reputation of not fully cooperating with those who carry out the study. Interviews have been limited to the female members of the households, who generally carry the burdens arising out of the high fertility in the family. Variables studied belong both to the Supply side and Demand side. A high degree of use of both prenatal and natal services has been observed in the study population. Integrated services of immunisation, family planning and maternal and child health have been offered, and the level of consumer satisfaction with services rendered seems to be high. Such a scenario provides an ideal opportunity for much more intensified efforts in family planning, and based on the trends available in the study, better results could be expected in the future. The data on communication reveals the crucial roles that satisfied adopters, friends and relatives can perform to influence couples to accept family planning practices. The association between female literacy and status with fertility has not been evident in this study, contrary to expectations. But it is well known that there are variables like monetary incentives that generally distort such relationships, particularly in slum populations. It is also possible that we need to know much more on the ingredients that really constitute status and modernisation among slum population; and more sophisticated tools for their measurement have to be devised. Inspite of these, the study as stated earlier, generally adds to the wealth of knowledge already available.

The study has been undertaken as part of her doctoral dissertation by the author. The Department of Population Studies, Sri Venkateswara University, has done well in promoting this study and it is hoped that many other departments like sociology, psychology, economics, public administration and anthropology will promote similar studies in the future, and thus add to the wealth of knowledge that will be useful in solving the population problem. Failure to achieve a rapid breakthrough in the population field will have serious and deleterious consequences to the nation and will adversely affect the quality of our present and future generation. The people of the country are intelligent but collective efforts to solve the problem are inadequate. The motto should be that "We Must Succeed" and no efforts should be spared in that direction.

Madras,

K.A. PISHAROTI
Population & Health
Consultant

CONTENTS

INTRODUCTION

The present research aims to study the various determinants of differential acceptance of family planning programme in the slum areas of Madras city. In this city, family planning programme began in a big way during early 1960's i.e., during the period of Sri R.A. Gopalasamy, whose dynamic leadership provided the necessary impetus to organise the first large-scale sterilisation programme in India. His pioneering efforts and experiments in vasectomy programme are well known. However, the programme did not get the same momentum for some time after his period. Nevertheless, during 1970's when Shri T.V. Antony was at the helm of affairs as Corporation Commissioner, the programme once again got necessary administrative support in Madras city. On the one side erratic enthusiasm of the Managers of the programme, and on the other hand apathy of public together led to poor performance of family planning programme in Madras city. Consequently the programme continues to suffer for want or dynamism and commitment in administration. Of course, the other major reason for the present poor performance of population control programme, stems out of the inadequate data base and knowledge on determinants of contraceptive behaviour. The present research is focussed on this theme.

No programme, leave alone family planning, can progress satisfactorily without a continuous backup of evaluation and periodic studies on determinants in the fluctuations of adoption of family planning. So far, in this city, only one major study was carried out by S. Chandrasekar in early 1950's on KAP of family planning. No doubt secondary data of Madras city was used by certain scholars to write the demographic profile of the city, but secondary data have several limitations in understanding the major determinants of non-acceptance of family planning among couples. This is the extent of gap of knowledge on family planning now existing in Madras city, which demands urgent attention to identify specific factors of non-contraception among various strata of urban population. It is needed in order to generate appropriate inputs for streamlining and strengthening the ongoing urban family planning programme in Madras city. Since, the rapid growth of population in Metropolitan city of Madras had started increasing at much faster rate than the amenities that could be offered to the people, there is once again urgent need for undertaking studies on determinants of family planning. Under these considerations the present research is innovative and a high priority scheme today.

Earlier Evidence : In the past, a few isolated efforts had been made by Demographers, Administrators and Health Educators to know the characteristics of sterilised persons belonging to slum and non-slum areas in Madras city and also in rural areas of Tamil Nadu. Out of them, the studies carried out by Chandrasekaran (1952), Agarwala (1962) Nair (1962), Nambiar (1966) and Antony (1975) constitute a few important contributions made on family planning programme of Madras city. While Chandrasekar, Agarwala and Nambiar focussed their study on knowledge, attitude and practice and the impact of family planning, the study by Antony and Nair covered mostly the characteristics of the sterilised persons besides the problem of post adoption complications, and motivations responsible for adoption and contraception. No doubt they have also covered aspects like socio-economic status, demographic profile and religious and caste background of the adopters.

In addition to these exclusive urban studies, a pioneering demographic effort was made in the peri-urban area of Madras Metropolitan area, viz., Mangadu village, by Chandrasekaran as early as in 1951. It was a study on trends, differentials and determinants of fertility among different cultural groups. This study confirmed the existing significance of differentials in fertility among the Caste Hindus, Harijans and Muslims. The same village was studied after a quarter century period by Aiyappan and Mahadevan (1988). This study interestingly proved that as a result of family planning and health programmes organised by the state government and the Poonamalee Public Health Institute, a significant decline in high fertility of the Harijans was achieved, which became almost equal to the traditionally low fertility of the Caste Hindus. Even the fertility of Muslims declined significantly. These authors attributed the achievements in fertility decline largely to the programme factors and to a certain extent to the influence of urbanization of the Madras city.

In addition to these studies, a few other efforts have also been made by the Gandhigram Institute of Rural Health and Family Planning in conducting family planning camps that were in vogue in different parts of the city as well as in rural areas of Thanjavur and Madurai districts during the 1970-1980 period. These evaluation studies gave priority to the study of characteristics of sterilised persons, their demographic effectiveness, post adoption problems and so on. Of course, the motivation and incentive aspects were also rightly covered in these studies (GIRH & FP, Bulletin, 1974).

Available meagre empirical evidence from these studies has confirmed that the existing infrastructural facilities are inadequate and whatever facilities are available could not be optimally utilised mainly because of several unknown constraints. The present strategy of the programme for promoting family planning acceptance is generally based on three distinct types of interventions. They are for providing: easily accessible contraceptive services; incentives or disincentives for acceptance of contraception; and education and persuasive communication to change the resistance. As observed by Ghosh (1978) and Jolley (1983), the present policy proposes a close monitoring of the programme performance, i.e., 'targets' under family welfare should be treated as milestones and yardsticks in the programmes. Hence, in actual practice the programme is highly target-oriented and its emphasis is on incentives. The communication component of the programme has to be revitalised at this juncture and this is possible by innovative studies to unravel the role played by the communication variables in contraceptive behaviour.

Chapters : This book consists of nine independent chapters with an introduction at the beginning. They have been organised on the following lines, viz., introduction, review of literature, methodology, an overview of family planning programme of Madras city, culture and contraceptive behaviour, socio-economic status, modernization and status of women, various inputs of the programme, communication and demographic variables. In Chapter 1, a number of Indian and International studies available on family planning acceptance and non-acceptance have been reviewed. The first step had been completed prior to the finalisation of this research design. It had been done with a view to make the present research more distinct and innovative from the earlier studies. The presentation is organised variable-wise and each variable is critically analysed for its relevance and importance for the present research. A variety of factors have been identified as directly or indirectly responsible for the contraceptive behaviour.

Chapter 2, Methodology, covers the details relating to research design, objectives, hypothesis, operational definition of terms, sample size and design, data collection procedure and data analysis. A number of major hypothesis have been tested. The sample consisted of 600 eligible couples (women) selected from the slum population. Both adopters and non-adopters were included in the study. A semi-structured schedule was used for data collection. Analysis was carried out using computer facility. By using tabulations and multivariate analysis interpretations were carried out. Important indices on autonomy in decision-making, women's roles, overall son preference and an index on satisfaction of service facilities were prepared and used for analysis. The total score value was graded and classified trichotomously and cross-tabulated with the contraceptive behaviour. A conceptual model on determinants of contraceptive decision-making developed by Mahadevan (1984), which is an appropriate scheme for the present study, has been adopted with necessary modifications.

Chapter 3 refers to the overview of Madras city slum and its family planning programme, demographic profile, administrative setup and organisation, achievement and the future prospects under the World Bank aided IPP-V programme. This project commenced in the Metropolitan city since 1985 and is presently engaged in implementation of family planning programme. This project envisages involvement of the several existing service centres, viz., child welfare centres, postpartum centres, and also the active involvement of all the voluntary organisations. This project also has several long-term and short-term objectives to work with reorganised pattern and with minimum worker population ratio for effective delivery system.

Chapter 4 refers to culture and contraceptive behaviour. The variables discussed are : religion, caste and value of sons. On the basis of religious background of the respondents, they have been cross-tabulated with the three distinct religious groups, viz., the Hindus, Muslims and Christians. On the basis of desire for sons, an attempt has been made to examine the influence of value of sons on contraceptive behaviour in the sample population. The contraceptive behaviour of the respondents has been analysed against the number of living sons also. In order to find out the cumulative importance of all dimensions of value of children, an index has been developed and used in the analysis.

Chapter 5 refers to socio-economic characteristics and contraceptive behaviour. The variables discussed in this chapter include : type of house, education of husband, education of wife and family annual income. This is to find out the importance of socio-economic status factors and their nature of influence on contraceptive behaviour.

Chapter 6 refers to modernisation and status of women in relation to contraceptive behaviour. Under this section, an attempt is made to know the level of modernisation of the respondents and their influence on family planning adoption by asking their opinions and experiences about various aspects of day-to-day life. The dimensions of modernization considered here are : religious tolerance, views on age at marriage (18 + years) of girls, belief in fortune telling, type of treatment preferred for children, and communication.

Chapter 7 deals with programme factors and contraceptive behaviour. Improving facilities and upgrading the technical quality of services will therefore be a major need for acceptance of family planning. In this context the present study has been highlighted with respect to the following programme variables : places of last delivery; persons attending to last delivery; types of health centres visited; types of staff, who gave services; types of services rendered; availability of service in acceptable manner; distance from places of treatment and opinion on incentives.

Interpersonal and mass media channels of family planning communication are focussed upon in Chapter 8. The communication variables considered here are : satisfied adopters, friends/ neighbours, relatives, dissatisfied adopters, family planning workers, voluntary workers and others, opinion on mass media channel and their satisfactory availability. The case studies and awareness on adopters and non-adopters, their success stories, failures and fear of adoption are also gathered and discussed here.

Demographic characteristics are dealt with in relation to contraceptive behaviour and presented in Chapter 9, the variables included under this chapter are : age of women, duration of marital life, number of living children and sex combination of children. At the end, a summary of the findings including the regression findings are given along with a few implications for the benefit of the future programme. The important factors that explained the determinants of contraception through regression analysis are : satisfactory service facilities : value of children, influence of satisfied adopters, and religious background of the couple. The · generalisations and programme implications discussed throughout this thesis will go a long way in understanding and predicting contraceptive behaviour, and for formulating new policies providing suitable and effective inputs to strengthen the ongoing family planning programme in metropolitan cities like Madras and in other developing countries.

CHAPTER 1

REVIEW OF LITERATURE

The study of factors influencing contraceptive behaviour assumes great importance in view of the high growth rate of population, which is a major problem faced by most of the developing countries, including India. The knowledge on various determinants of contraceptive behaviour may contribute to the advancement of precise theoretical conceptualization and policy formulation in the field of family planning programme. In this field, so far, a number of factors have been identified as directly or indirectly responsible for the adoption of contraception. They include a number of socio-economic, demographic, cultural, ecological, health and other input variables responsible for the adoption or non-adoption of family planning. Though these studies have identified considerable factors responsible for contraceptive behaviour, knowledge is not adequate for fully explaining the major causes for the performance of family planning programme in slum areas, where the growth of population is very high. Therefore in order to take stock of the status of determinants of adoption and non-adoption of contraception, an attempt is made in this Chapter to review the existing literature relating to this problem.

I. Religion and Caste

(i) *Religion :* Religion is one of the important cultural factors that determine the contraceptive behaviour of the people. It plays a crucial role in forming the values, attitudes and action of people regarding family planning. Some of the studies conducted all over the world (Kirk, 1966, Gavin and Dorothy, 1968; Presser and Bumpass, 1970; Hein, 1977) have shown that fertility levels were higher among the Muslims as compared to the Christians and thereby indicating lower rate of adoption of family planning among the Muslims than the Christians. Kirk (1966) has observed that Muslim fertility throughout the world has been almost universally high, the range of crude birth rate being between 40 to 60 per thousand population. In contrast, Roman Catholic countries have birth rates that are one of the highest in Latin American countries, but the lowest in Europe (Gavin and Dorothy, 1968). Another study conducted by the Korean Institute of Family Planning (1979) reveals that 'religious' women are practising contraception more than 'irreligious' people. However, among the religious women, greater proportion of Catholics practise family planning than the Buddhists and Protestants. Therefore we see a contradiction in the influence of religion on family planning.

A survey conducted in Mauritius by Hein (1977) reported that the percentage of these never using contraception was higher among the Hindus (41%) followed by the Muslims (37%) and the lowest among the Christians (28%). In another study among women aged 15-35 in the urban area of Illorium, Nigeria, Oni and McCharthy (1986) observed that the Christians were more likely to have used or be currently using contraceptives than Muslim women. Interestingly, Davis (1967) and Notestin et al., (1968) argued that the religious axioms themselves are not important for the problem of accepting birth control methods. Their view is that what is needed is the changes in basic values of religion and reorientation of these values to meet new requirement of behavioural change.

In India, most of the studies (Som and Sengupta, 1960; Sarupria 1964; Kurup, 1968; ORG, 1972; Mukherjee, 1973; Siddha, 1974; Hemalatha et al., 1977; Srivastava, 1978; Rele and Kanitkar, 1980; Kanitkar and Murthy, 1983; Danda 1984; Bhate, 1984; Audinarayana, 1986 and Government of India, 1986) have conclusively proved that the Christians in general, were more favourably inclined and used one or the other methods of family planning, followed by the Hindus and the Muslims. Based on an extensive study in rural and urban West Bengal, Som and Sengupta (1960) concluded that "in general Hindu respondents appeared to be more disposed towards family planning and contraception than Muslims". For instance, they found that among the rural Hindu respondents, 60 per cent of them favoured limiting family size and 44 per cent favoured the use of contraceptives whereas among the Muslims these proportions were only 24 and 13 respectively. In Kerala, based on his experience, Kurup (1968) concluded that the proportion of Muslims among sterilized persons was much smaller than their proportion in the general population.

Findings from an All India Study (ORG, 1972) revealed that the practice of family planning was higher among the Christians and Parsis (30%), followed by the Hindus (19%) and lastly by the Muslims (13%). These differences among the religious groups were also statistically significant. In Bhiwandi area of Thane District, Maharashtra, Srivastava (1978) found that the percentage of women currently practising family planning was higher among the Hindus (35%) as compared to the Muslims (22%). In Greater Bombay, according to a fertility and family planning survey, Rele and Kanitkar observed that the rate of practice of family planning was the highest among the Zoroastrians (70%), followed by the Hindus (25%), other Christians (20%), Muslims (18%) and the lowest among the Roman Catholics (9%). Bhate (1984) in rural Maharashtra, noticed that the acceptance of sterilisation and other contraceptive was very low among the Muslims than among the Hindus. Similarly, in a recent study of rural Andhra Pradesh, Audinarayana (1986) found that the percentage of adoptions was slightly higher among the Hindus (40%) than among the Muslims (37%). Another recent study undertaken by the Government of India (1986) in 16 States of India, reported that the percentage of family planning acceptors were higher among the Christians (80%), followed by the Hindus (62%) and the Muslims (60%). Thus the preceding evidence has conclusively established that there exist significant differentials in contraceptive behaviour by the religious background of the concerned persons. Therefore, in the present study religion of the respondent has been considered as one of the independent variables influencing contraceptive behaviour.

(ii) *Caste :* Caste is one of the major stratification variables in India, which may affect the attitude towards and adoption of family planning methods. Generally, higher caste people may have better socio-economic status, which may lead to higher level of adoption of family planning as compared to the backward and scheduled castes. Several studies in India, have exhibited a higher rate of family planning adoption among the upper caste groups followed by the backward castes and the comparatively much lower rate of adoption noticed among the scheduled castes (Karlin, 1968; Shatkawat, et al., 1974; Kaur, 1974; Mahadevan, 1979; Ghosal and Sarkar, 1983; Audinarayana, 1986; Rao et al., 1986; Shakilarani, 1989).

Findings from a study conducted in 8 villages in Maharashtra, Andhra Pradesh and West Bengal (Karlin, 1968), suggested that the caste of the respondents was positively and significantly associated with their knowledge, approval and adoption of vasectomy and loop. Shatkawat et al., 1974 observed that acceptance of contraception was highest among the upper caste groups. A study conducted by Kaur (1974) about family planning in two Industrial Units at Faridabad, revealed that adoption of family planning was highest among the middle caste male and female respondents from Escorts as well as Bata Factories. It declined slightly in case of upper castes but the scheduled caste groups had the lowest adoption rates in both the factories. While observing a higher family planning adoption among upper caste members as against lower caste groups in rural areas of Madurai District in Tamil Nadu, Mahadevan (1979) argued that "the means through which the upper caste regulate their child birth are by means of induced abortion, voluntary and involuntary abstinence and reducing coital frequency. All these methods are not popular among the lower caste groups."

In Bihar, Ghosal and Sarkar (1983) found that the family planning acceptance was higher among the upper caste groups and lower among the scheduled caste groups. Based on the study conducted in three districts, in Karnataka, Rao et al., (1986) reported a higher acceptance rate among upper caste groups and lower practice of contraception among those belonging to lower castes. For example, the acceptance rate was high among Lingayats (higher caste group—47%), whereas it was low (7%) among the Kuruba caste (lower caste people). A recent study by Audinarayana (1986) in rural Andhra Pradesh and Shakilarani (1989) in a Tamil Nadu village have also recorded that the percentage of family planning acceptors is higher among the forward caste groups followed by the backward castes and lowest among the scheduled castes. Hence this variable is also taken into consideration in the present study as one of the cultural factors.

II. Demographic Variables

The influence of demographic variables, viz., age at marriage and present age of women and number of living children on contraceptive behaviour are considered here for discussion. Most of the studies reviewed under this section have taken into consideration one or the other of these demographic variables, but not all these variables together.

(i) *Age at Marriage of Women :* Age at marriage of females is a starting point in the reproductive process, which is traditionally low in developing countries like India. It is a well known fact that higher age at marriage helps in controlling fertility by shortening the reproduction span as well as through the shift in fertility pattern towards fewer children in women's later years. Higher age at marriage is partly attributable to factors like education and modernization (Agarwala, 1965). In the context of contraceptive behaviour, increase in age at marriage increases the female education, develops modern outlook, enables understanding of the importance of small family, which may increase their awareness, knowledge, interest and create favourable attitude towards family planning methods.

Though age at marriage is recognised as a major demographic variable, only a few researchers have discussed it as an independent variable to explain the variations in family planning behaviour. Morrison (1956), in a village of Maharashtra, found that age at marriage was directly related to the favourable attitude to family planning. Similarly, a study among the Muslims (Fatima, 1977) also showed a positive relationship between wives' age at marriage and attitude to family planning. Bhatia (1984) also pointed out that among the rural Ghana women (West Africa), there exists a positive association between the wives' age at marriage and knowledge about family planning.

Regarding the influence of age at marriage on contraceptive behaviour, a few studies have conclusively proved that there exists a significant positive association between the wives' age at marriage and the adoption of family planning (Bhatia, 1979; Audinarayana, 1981; 1986; 1987; Sivaraju, 1982; Arora, 1983; Bhatia, 1983; Bhuyan and Bhuyan, 1984; Rajaratnam, 1986; Shakilarani, 1989). Bhatia (1979), Arora (1983) and Audinarayana (1987) have noticed a significant positive association between the female age at marriage and overall couple protection rates pertaining to the different states in India. Audinarayana (1986) in his rural Andhra Pradesh study, noticed that the percentage of family planning adoptors increased from a lower level of 33 to a higher level of 52, as the wives' age at marriage increased from 13 or less to 18 years and above. Further, this pattern is almost same among the Caste Hindus and the Harijans but somewhat negative and inconsistent among the Muslims. In a rural area of Tamil Nadu, Rajaratnam (1986) found that the ever users of contraception was 37 per cent among those who married at age 17 or below and it was above 40 per cent for those married at age 18 or above. Similarly, one of the very recent studies in a Tamil Nadu village (Shakilarani, 1989) has also concluded that age at marriage of females will have a significant positive influence on the current use of contraception.

(ii) *Age of Women :* Age of women is a demographic variable which determines fertility, mortality, migration and also use of contraception. In the field of family planning, it has a pivotal role because it is highly relevant for the couple as long as wife remains in the reproductive period. In the early seventies, people from the higher age groups came forward for sterilization. With the impact of family planning education and incentives offered to the clients, it became possible to attract younger people especially those who had already acquired the desired number of children. A number of studies, so far, carried out in India and abroad have established that the use of contraceptive will be very low in the early ages, it increases in the middle ages and again falls in the older ages (U.N., 1961; I.I.P.O. 1964; Caldwell, 1968; Swee-Hock, 1968; Presser and Bumpass, 1970; ORG, 1972; Mukherjee, 1973; Rahman et al., 1980; Rele and Kanitkar, 1980; Sooradji and Hatmadji, 1981; Bhatia, 1982; Reddy, 1984; Zachariah, 1984; Sathar and Chidambaram, 1984; Rao et al., 1986; Oni and McCharthy 1986; Shakilarani, 1989).

In rural Kenya, Caldwell (1968) found that women who were presently using contraceptives were on an average older than those who had never done so and thus concluded that the practice is likely to be more continuous among older women and presumably those of higher parity. Likewise, Swee-Hock (1968) also reported that "the proportion of wives who have ever used birth control, increased slowly with the advance of age from ten to fourteen per cent." In Bangladesh, Rahaman et al., (1980) observed that the contraceptive acceptance rates and rate of current use increased through 30-34 age group, remained fairly stable through the 35-39 age group and then declined substantially. According to Sooradji and Hatmadji (1981) in Indonesia, "the current use increases with age, until it reaches a peak of 4 per cent at the ages of 30-34, remains high between 35 and 44 and then declines". Based on the data from 28 developing countries (World Fertility Survey Data), Sathar and Chidambaram (1984) arrived at the conclusion that "During the early part of the reproductive life, the incidence of contraceptive use is low, it increases in the middle ages and again falls at the older ages." More or less, similar type of association between the present age of women and use of contraceptives was noticed in the countries of Malaysia (Peng and Abdurahman, 1981), Bangladesh (Bhatia, 1982) and Nigeria (Oni and McCharthy, 1986).

In India, some of the studies have exhibited the above noticed trend between the age of women and use of contraceptives, whereas some others have expressed a positive association between these two variables. For example, findings from Mysore Population Study (U.N. 1961) suggested that the use of family planning methods increased with age of women. However, based on an all India rural-urban survey, Indian Institute of Public Opinion (1964) highlighted that there exists an inverse relationship between the age of women and practice of family planning. But a significant positive association was observed by Operations Research Group, Baroda (1972) and Mukherjee (1973) in their studies.

An empirical study by Zachariah (1984) in Kerala showed that the practice of family planning increased with the age upto 35 years, after which it decreased. For example, the percentage of ever married women currently using conventional family planning methods was 7.8 in the age group of 15-19, which has increased to 21.1 for 20-24 years and then to 21.3 for 25-29 years, but thereafter it declined to 19.5, 18.2, 19.1, and 15.5 respectively as age of women increased to 30-34, 35-39, 40-44 and 45-49 respectively. More or less, similar findings were also noticed by Rao et al., (1986) in three Districts of Karnataka (Kaur et al., 1986), in eight villages of Haryana and also by Shakilarani (1989) in a Tamil Nadu village.

(iii) *Number of Living Children :* The number of living children seems to be an important demographic variable in influencing the adoption of family planning. Couples who have achieved the desired or the preferred number of children will be in a better position to accept family planning than those who have yet to achieve the desired number of children. Further, a married individual's status in society can be enhanced only when an individual has many children because childlessness of an individual has traditionally been regarded as one of the greatest misfortunes. Under these circumstances, we may expect a positive association between the number of living children and use of contraception. Most of the studies conducted both in India and all over the world have established this fact (Agarwala, 1961; Karlin, 1968; Sengupta, 1969; ORG, 1972; Kaur, 1974; Khan, 1979; Rele and Kanitkar, 1980; Sivaraju, 1982; Danda, 1984; Reddy, 1984; Bertrand et al., 1985; Oni and McCharthy, 1986 and Chandra, 1987).

In rural Zaire, Brown and Brown (1980) observed that the percentage of acceptors of family planning was the highest among those who have four living children (71%) followed by 48 and 36 per cent respectively among those who have three and two living children, whereas the corresponding percentage among those who have only one child was 28 per cent only. In another rural study Baszaire, Bertrand, et al., (1985) also observed that there exists a positive (at .001 per cent level) correlation between practice of family planning and number of living children. Similarly, Oni and McCharthy (1986) in Nigeria, noticed that the 'contraceptive use is positively associated with the number of living children'.

A few researchers in India also reported the existence of direct association between the number of living children and adoption of contraception. In villages near Delhi, Agarwala (1961) found that the use of contraceptives and willingness to learn increased when the number of living children increased to five or more. According to Kivlin (1968), in eight villages of Maharashtra, Andhra Pradesh and West Bengal, respondents with large number of living children were more likely to use family planning than with fewer living children. More or less, similar positive association was noticed by Sengupta (1969) in Calcutta, ORG, Baroda (1972) at all India level, Kaur (1974) in two industrial units at Delhi and Khan (1974) among the Muslims of Kanpur city, Uttar Pradesh.

Based on the Greater Bombay Fertility and Family Planning Survey, Rele and Kanitkar (1980) indicated that there exists a direct relationship between the rate of current contraceptive practice and number of living children. Similar type of consistent positive association was also observed by Reddy (1984) in rural Andhra Pradesh, Danda (1984) at Basudha Village in Burdwan District of West Bengal and Chandra (1987) in rural and urban areas of Delhi. Thus, almost all the studies mentioned in this section have conclusively proved that the number of living children will play a significant role in determining the contraceptive behaviour. Hence, this variable i.e., number of living children has been considered here as one of the independent variables, to examine whether it has any influence on the use of contraceptives among the slum population in Madras city.

III. Value of Children

Value of children plays an important role in the field of family planning. Value of children is more in developing countries as compared to developed countries. Schultz (1973) rightly pointed out that the 'children are very important in the sense that they form poor man's capital'. Some of the studies observed the following value dimensions for desiring male and more number of children : 1. for religious reasons, 2. expansion of self and immortality, 3. primary group ties and affiliation, 4. fun and happiness, 5. power and influence, and 6. pride of accomplishment and sense of excellence over others (U.N. 1961; Caldwell, 1967; Poffenberger and Poffenberger, 1971; Arnold, 1975; Khan, 1979). Caldwell (1968) writes "the large family system is buttressed by three main causes. Children are either economically valuable or at least share the work burden, they provide assistance much needed in societies without Governmental social services during old age and to a lesser extent sickness; and they add by their numbers to the parental prestige".

Though in general children are valued, sons are generally preferred in the traditional and rural societies. Freedman (1968) concludes that sons in present day societies are considered to have economic utility in terms of assistance in agricultural production and provision of security in parental old age. Kirk (1966) found that among Muslim population, sons are viewed as having religious utility through their religious intervention before and after death. In Pakistan, Robert et al., (1965) noticed that among the 69 couples with children but without any male child, greater proportion desired additional children before accepting contraception. They also found that couples with three or more living children are over-represented among the adopters and early adopters had more living children than later adopters.

Preference for sons for many purposes is also most predominant in India. Mamdani (1972) is of the view that the strong preference for sons stems from a variety of social, economic and religious reasons and every family in India aspires for at least one son. Similarly, in a study conducted by Sharma et al., (1974), it is stated that most of the wives believe that one must have a son mainly to carry on the lineage and to support the family. Some of the studies have proved the influence of son preference on the adoption of family planning (Morrison, 1956; Goode, 1963; Poffenberger,

1968; Kaur, 1974; Khan, 1979; Rele and Kanitkar, 1980; Sivaraju, 1982; Reddy, 1984; Reddy, 1985; Shakilarani, 1989). In eight villages of Maharashtra, Andhra Pradesh and West Bengal, Karlin (1968) noticed that families with two or more living sons were more likely to practice family planning than those with fewer sons. Kaur (1974) in two industrial units at Delhi observed that there existed a highly positive and significant association between the level of family planning adoption and number of male living children. More or less similar consistent positive association between the number of sons and use of contraceptives was also found in Kanpur city, Uttar Pradesh (Khan, 1979), in Greater Bombay (Rele and Kanitkar, 1980), in rural urban Andhra Pradesh (Sivaraju, 1982; Reddy, 1984; Reddy, 1985) and in a Tamil Nadu village (Shakilarani, 1989). Thus, most of the studies reviewed above fully confirmed the strong relationship between the various dimensions of value of children (including son preference) and contraceptive behaviour. A nationwide study recently conducted by Mahadevan (1988) confirmed the principal importance of value of children as the most important determinant of fertility behaviour in U.P., A.P. and Kerala states. However, its importance was greater in U.P. and A.P. and much less in Kerala. Hence, in the present study, this variable has been considered as a major independent variable.

IV. Socio-Economic Variables

Of all the factors influencing the contraceptive behaviour, socio-economic status variables occupy a pivotal position. Traditionally it is a well-known fact that there exists a positive association between the socio-economic status variables and adoption of family planning. However, in the recent past this positive relationship is relatively disturbed due to the influence of urbanization, industrialisation and social change. But Reddy (1984) in a recent survey of Hyderabad city slum and non-slum population, noticed a linear positive relationship between socio-economic status (index) measured by the respondents' education, occupation and household income, and adoption of contraceptives. Since socio-economic status is a complex variable, an attempt is made to highlight some of the studies which have focussed on the individual characteristics of socio-economic status.

(i) *Education* : In general, higher educational status increases the knowledge and changes the attitude towards family planning, which, in turn, leads to the use of contraceptives. Several studies conducted around the world have reported a positive association between the educational status and the adoption of family planning methods (Rainwater, 1965; Whelpton et al., 1966; Barbara et al., 1981; Sathar and Chidambaram, 1984; Murthy and DeVos, 1988; Oni and McCharthy, 1986). Rainwater (1965) and Whelpton et al., (1966) inferred that 'while some form of fertility limitation is nearly universal in the United States, wives with little formal education are less likely to use contraceptives especially in the early stage of family formation'. Brown and Brown (1980) in their study at rural Zaire found that well-educated African couples accepted modern contraception in greater proportion (27%), whereas less-educated couples accept it the least (10%). Based on the analysis of World Fertility Survey Data for 28 countries, Sathar and Chidambaram (1984) concluded that "The pattern is very clear; the higher the number of years of schooling, greater is the prevalence of contraceptive use". Of the 28 countries, Fiji is the only exception where the level of use is not found to vary with the length of period of schooling". Murthy and De Vos (1985) observed in Sri Lanka, that there exists a significant positive association between educational level of women and contraceptive use, irrespective of their ethnic background.

In India also several studies have reported a positive association between the educational status and the adoption of family planning methods (Som and Sengupta 1960, Muleitha and Kaur, 1962; U.N., 1961 ; Sarupriya, 1964; Jha et al., 1969; Nayar and George, 1972; ORG, 1972; Mukherjee, 1973; Kaur, 1974, Khan, 1979; Rele and Kanitkar, 1980; Danda, 1984; Zachariah, 1984; Rao et al., 1986; Kaur, et al., 1988; Shakilarani, 1989). In the pioneering Mysore Population Study (U.N., 1961), it was highlighted that use of family limitation methods increased with educational status. Findings from Chetla Urban Health Centre, Calcutta (Muleitha and Kaur, 1962) confirmed that education of husband has a profound positive impact of family planning adoption. For example, among illiterate husbands, the practice of family planning was only 19 per cent as against 34 per cent among those with secondary and higher education. Similarly, Sarupriya (1964) found that in a district town near Jaipur, the percentage in favour of family planning among illiterates was 38, while it was 62 among those with primary education. For those who have secondary and college education, the percentages in favour of family planning were 57 and 70 respectively.

Based on an "All India Study", ORG, Baroda (1972) concluded that the effect of education of family planning practice was significant at 1 per cent level. More or less, similar direct relationships between the educational status and adoption of family planning was also noticed in rural and urban areas of Haryana and Tamil Nadu (Mukherjee, 1973), in two industrial units (ESCORTS and BATA FACTORIES) of Faridabad near Delhi (Kaur, 1974) in Kanpur city (Khan, 1979) Greater Bombay (Rele and Kanitkar, 1980) and also in two different regions of Andhra Pradesh.

Singh and Gupta (1983) in their case study of Patna observed that education is significantly related to sterilization. For example, the percentage of adopters were more (79%) among those educated upto matriculation and above as compared to those educated below matriculation level (21%). Rao et al., (1986) in their rural study of three districts in Karnataka also found that education had a positive effect on the adoption of family planning. For instance, in Dakshina Kannada District, the practice of contraception was comparatively higher (32%) for the husbands educated upto middle school whereas it was lower (26%) for those educated upto primary level, and least for the illiterates (21%). When women's education is taken into consideration the corresponding percentages among those who are at higher, primary and illiterate levels were 39, 31 and 23 respectively. Further, they concluded that education is one of the most important determinants of contraceptive use especially in the use of temporary methods. More or less similar pattern was also observed by Kaur et al., (1988) in eight villages of Haryana State and also by Shakilarani (1989) in a Tamil Nadu village. Thus, almost all the aforesaid studies revealed that there exists a positive relationship between educational status and adoption of family planning. Hence, in the present study also this variable has been considered as one of the major socio-economic status variables to examine its influence on the contraceptive behaviour.

(ii) *Occupation :* Occupation of a person is one of the good indicators to measure the socio-economic status. Generally, higher occupational status is associated with higher education and income, which, in turn, leads to higher rate of adoption of family planning methods. Some of the studies conducted in different countries of the world have established that the rate of adoption of family planning will be higher among working as against non-working, among non-agricultural workers and among white-collared higher professionals as compared to lower professional workers (Fisek et al., 1968, K I F P, 1979; Brown and Brown, 1980; Tsui et al., 1981; Knodel, et al., 1984; Sathar and Chidambaram, 1984; Abdullah et al., 1986; Oni and McCharthy, 1986). Brown and Brown (1980) in rural Zaire found that the proportion of 'white-collar' worker (Clerks, Teachers, Nurses) was probably somewhat higher among acceptor husbands than among the general population, which reveals the higher family planning acceptance among the white-collared workers.

While analysing the data collected in the World Fertility Survey of Bangladesh, Korea and Mexico Tsui et al., (1981) noticed that there exists a strong positive association between social class (occupation) and contraceptive use. For instance, the rates of contraceptive use were lowest for the wives of the farmer class (8.6, 42.7 and 15.1 in respective countries) whereas the corresponding rates were much higher for the wives of non-manual workers (21.2, 61.6 and 55.3 respectively). However, Sathar and Chidambaram (1984) did not find any consistent pattern between work status of women and contraceptive use, in 28 developing countries. Interestingly, looking at the differentials in contraceptive use by occupation of their husbands they arrived at the following conclusions : "Invariably, the use of contraception is highest among the wives of men engaged in professional and clerical occupations. At the other end of the spectrum, women whose husbands report no work are less likely to use contraception than those engaged in work, but there are many exceptions to this — Malaysia, Thailand, Haiti, Syria, Kenya, Bangladesh, Sudan, Pakistan and Nepal.

Several states in India also have confirmed the above patterns of relationships between occupational status and adoption of family planning (Jacob Paul, 1965; Goyal, 1965; Sengupta and Roy, 1969; ORG, 1972; Mukherjee, 1973; Kaur, 1974; Khan, 1979; Rele and Kanitkar, 1980; Sivaraju, 1982; Kanitkar and Murthy, 1983; Singh and Gupta, 1983; Danda, 1984; Shakilarani, 1989). Jacob Paul (1965) in his study in Hoogly District of West Bengal, found that among those who are engaged in skilled and technical works, the percentage of acceptance of family planning was 7 per cent, whereas among the unskilled and manual workers it was 28 per cent. However, among those who are in trade and business, the acceptance rate was only 5 per cent but among the cultivators, this percentage was much higher (43%). Based on an experimental family planning project near Calcutta city, Sengupta and Roy (1969) revealed that in experimental area, the percentage of adopters among the manual workers was the lowest (35%) but the same increased to 40 per cent among the technical workers and further increased to 42 per cent among the professional groups. The corresponding proportions in the controlled area were 33, 53 and 56 respectively. In an "All India Study" by ORG, Baroda (1972) showed that the practice of family planning was lowest among the skilled/unskilled manual workers, whereas it was highest among the professionals. However, a further two-way analysis of variance considering educational level of husband and occupation simultaneously showed that the effects of occupation were not statistically significant. More or less, similar pattern was also noticed by Mukherjee (1973), Kaur (1974) and Khan (1979) in their respective studies.

In Greater Bombay, according to a Fertility and Family Planning Survey, Rele and Kanitkar (1980) observed that the highest use of contraception was noticed among wives working in administrative, professional and technical cadres (53%) followed by clerical (38%) and sales professions (38%); whereas the lowest rates were observed among the house-wives (23%) and also among those women who are engaged in other skilled or unskilled work and primary sector. Singh and Gupta (1983) in their case study of Patna also observed that the higher the level of occupation, greater the rate of adoption and further they found a significant correlation between these two variables. Based on these studies, it may be concluded that differential occupational status of both the husbands as well as wives will lead to significant differentials in contraceptive use. Hence, in this study also occupational status of both the husbands and wives has been considered as independent variable to see its nature of relationship with the adoption of contraceptives.

(iii) *Economic Status :* Economic status of the family is a good indicator of socio-economic status. Several studies conducted in India and abroad conclusively proved that there exists a positive association between the economic status of a person (couples) and use of contraceptives (Agarwala, 1961; U.N., 1961; Muleitha and Kaur, 1962; Sarupria, 1964; Rainwater, 1960, 1965; ORG, 1972: Mukherjee, 1973; Kaur, 1974; Carvajal and Gaithman, 1976; Khan, 1979, Singh and Gupta, 1983, Government of India, 1986; Shakilarani, 1989). Rainwater (1960, 1965) and Whelpton et al., (1966) from their studies inferred that in the United States, lower class people have more children than the middle and upper classes.

Lower class fertility appears to be higher due to the insufficient and ineffective use of contraception. Based on their study in seven Latin American countries, Carvajal and Gaithman (1976) remarked that "not only does the use of contraception tend to increase with the level of income, but also adoption of more sophisticated contraceptive techniques is more likely to occur among higher income couples".

In India, the pioneering Mysore Population Study (U.N., 1961) reported that "the economic status is positively related to the practice of family planning." Muleitha and Kaur (1962) in their Chetla Urban Health Centre Study, noticed that among the higher income group, 57 per cent of wives were practising family planning, while this percentage was very low among the lower income group (20%). Similarly in Singur Rural Health Centre area near Calcutta the same researches found that 33 per cent of those with monthly income exceeding Rs. 150 practised family planning as compared to 22 per cent in lower income group. A well established positive association between the family income and practice of family planning was noticed in one of the studies conducted by ORG in the All India Survey (ORG, 1978). For example, over 50 per cent of the couples with family income of over Rs. 1,000 per month had ever practised family planning as against 13 per cent in the lowest income group of Rs. 100 per month or below. However, based on a study of Haryana and Tamil Nadu, Mukherjee (1973) remarked that while the monthly household expenditure has very low correlation with practice of any family planning method in Haryana , a moderate correlation (Sig. at .01 level) between these two variables was found in Tamil Nadu.

Interestingly, a highly positive and significant association was observed between the income and the level of family planning adoption by Kaur (1974) in two industrial units near Delhi and also by Khan (1974) among the Muslims of Kanpur city. From study conducted in three localities of Patna, Singh and Gupta (1983) inferred that respondents belonging to the higher income categories are more inclined to sterilization than those belonging to the lower income group. The mean monthly income for the adopters was calculated at Rs. 565 whereas for the non-adopters, it was only Rs. 47. The association was further supported by the significant values of 't' ratio (t = 2.5 df = 198, significant at 0.005 level). Thus, almost all the studies discussed in this section have conclusively proved that there exists a significant positive association between the economic status and adoption of family planning. Therefore, this variable has been taken as one of the independent variables influencing contraceptive behaviour for the present study.

V. Family Planning Communication

Communication plays a predominant role in the field of family planning. Among different methods of communication, inter-personal communication is generally found to be more effective in propagating information about family planning than the other channels of communication. In developed countries due to modernisation and high socio-economic status, communication plays a greater role, which makes people more rational in their outlook to discuss freely about contraception. In this section, a few studies which have focussed on the influence of various channels of communication in relation to adoption of family planning have been discussed at length.

Interpersonal Communication

Several studies (Saxena, 1965, Pillai, 1971; Gopalan, 1971) reported that neighbours, friends, relatives and other informal sources form the major sources of information on family planning. Health and Family Planning Workers are not a frequent source of information according to a few studies (Pethe, 1959; Chandrasekaran and Barbara, 1963) while other studies indicate them as major sources (Arora, 1966; Anand, 1967; Pillai, 1968). While some studies reported relatives as a source of information in decision-making (Pillai, 1968, 1971), others (Govindachari, 1967) reported that relatives play a less important source of information for men. Canvassers were also found to be effective by Repetto (1966) and Pillai (1968). A few studies also reported local leaders as an effective force in decision-making (Pillai, 1968, 1971). Friends and relatives were more often reported as a source of information for permanent methods (Govindachari, 1967). Satisfied users as an effective source of information have been mentioned by some of the researchers like Mahadevan (1984), Vasa (1967), Mandke (1968), Bhagar et al., (1968) and Chowdhary et al., (1972), Mahadevan et al., (1977) proved that the satisfied adopters are the most important and successful change agents in promoting family planning. Gopalan and Nayar (1969) also argued that the use of acceptors as promoters yield good results in getting more clients. A study conducted by the Department of Statistics, University of Kerala (1967) concluded that the most effective means of reaching eligible couples is through house-to-house canvassing.

Intra-spouse Communication

Husband-wife communication is an important factor in the field of family planning communication because spouses are the major parties to decide about their family size. Sufficient evidence exists from the studies conducted abroad to substantiate the dominance and the segregation roles which may affect the decision of the husband and wife jointly to practise family planning. (Stycos et al., 1954; Hill et al., 1959; Michel, 1967; Weller, 1968; Lieu et al., 1970; U.N. 1974). Michel (1967) in his study of 'Interaction in the French Urban family' found that equality or wife dominance among the couple were directly related to the couple's realization of the goals of family planning. Also, the more frequently there was equality or wife dominance, the more frequently had the couple avoided excessive fertility. These data agree with the findings of a Puerto Rican Study by Hill et al., (1959). Lieu et al., (1970) in their study of husband-wife relationship among couples in Philippine found that greater equality and affection between husband and wife were associated with both lower family size desires and higher contraceptive efficacy, even when socio-economic status is controlled. In Puerto Rico, Weller (1958) also found that while the knowledge of contraception was not related to the type of family decision-making, its effective use was greater among couples with less dominant husbands.

Studies conducted in India (Arora, 1966; Dubey and Goldein, 1967; Poffenberger, 1969; Sengupta, 1969; Pillai, 1971; U.N., 1975; Mukherjee, 1975; Khan, 1979; Sivaraju, 1987; Shakilarani, 1989) have also indicated a significant positive association between husband-wife communication and the adoption of family planning. Arora (1966), in her study of 70 women who had accepted IUD from the Central Government Dispensary at Laxmibai Nagar, New Delhi, observed that in most cases, it was mostly husband and wife, who had made the decision jointly. In almost all the cases, the other family members were not even aware of the decision. Among the urban middle class couples in New Delhi, Dubey and Goldein (1967) observed that the dominance of the husband precludes the wife taking an equal part in the decision-making and consequently effective practice of contraception becomes a much more difficult task than where the decision to prastice contraception is mutually agreed upon. Based on a study conducted in Calcutta City, Sengupta (1969) concluded that there was significant relationship between practice of family planning and spouses' communication. For example, of the 43 per cent who did not practice contraception 2 per cent had no communication between spouses whereas out of the 47 per cent who currently practised it, 44 per cent of them had communicated on different topics of family planning.

Khan (1979) inferred that the best source of family planning information for females is their husbands. He also found that husband-wife communication and empathy played an important role in the adoption of family planning. A significant association between reference group attitude towards contraception as perceived by the husband and the acceptance of family planning was observed. Similarly based on a study conducted in two extreme regions of Andhra Pradesh, Rayalaseema and Coastal Andhra, Sivaraju (1987) found significant relationship between husband and wife communication on family planning and contraceptive acceptance (at 1% level). Further, he mentioned that intra-spouse communication on family planning was greater among adopters than non-adopters of contraception in both regions. Data from a village of Tamil Nadu (Shakilarani, 1989) also confirmed that the percentage of current users was significantly (at .001 level) higher among those women who discussed with their husbands as compared to those who did not discuss with their husbands, irrespective of the number of children they possess.

Mass Media

Communication through mass media plays an important role in the field of family planning. Though all types of mass media such as Telephones, Mailings, Newspapers, Films, Radios and Televisions are prevalent in developed countries, the prevalence and the influence of only three sources like Newspaper, Films and Radio mostly exist in developing countries including India. In recent years, family planning organisations have used newspapers in a variety of ways as a medium for disseminating family planning stories. It was also used for advertisements ranging from a few lines in classified sections to full page advertisements, and in advertising campaigns to support the commercial distribution of contraceptives. The advantages of newspapers are that they form a highly visible medium. Often it is considered authoritative by a section of the readers and have a predetermined readership based on circulation pattern and even have secondary readership.

Sweeney (1977) on the basis of studies conducted in 22 countries has rightly concluded as follows : "Advertisements in Newspapers offer material on contraceptives sufficiently to warrant continuing progress in India, Sri Lanka, Taiwan. In one case, there is evidence of increase in clinic attendance after heavy use of newspapers in a campaign carried out in Ghana and a fairly high recall of press advertisements observed after a campaign in Nigeria. On the other hand, press advertisements resulted in low recall of family planning information in a number of studies which examined newspapers as a source of information in India, Iran and Korea. Newspapers did not impress particularly in most cases. However, there was a correlation between urbanization and socio-economic status and higher newspaper readership in Korea. Also in India, Sri Lanka and Korea men identified newspapers as a source of information more than women.

In Japan, the First Survey conducted by the Mainichi Group of Newspapers (1950) showed that 50 per cent of the respondents approved of contraception and about 20 per cent were practising contraception when they read newspaper advertisement on contraception. By 1963, 90 per cent recognised the concept of planned births and the practice rate was 44 per cent. At the same time, the ideal number of children was moving from three to two children. In Korea also, studies (ASI Market Research INC. 1974, Kwon et al., 1970) showed that newspaper form a primary source of information particularly among urban, educated men and women. For the commercial distribution of condoms in Sri Lanka newspapers were included as part of its promotion programme on marketing (Population Service International, 1976). The volume of film materials in the family planning area is considerable, and yet there is a surprising paucity of solid research material about their quality, distribution and effectiveness. Sweeney (1977) reviewing the studies related to films as mentioned above concluded that a large number of people used to attend the movies, particularly in Hong Kong, Iran, Philippines and Taiwan. In India, movie-goers are largely the urban and rural middle class population. Studies of audience recall of films and film messages show 8 per cent recall in

Taiwan, 15-24 per cent in India and 8 per cent recall in Iran. The Iranian Fast Campaign survey owed that persons who had been to the movies within the preceding 90 days had a very high recall of a filmstrip and its contraceptive message.

Among the first media used in family planning, radio is especially important due to its capacity to reach over great geographical distances and to convey information to illiterate people. Park (1967) in the post campaign survey conducted in Korea infers that "Radio ranked first as a source of information ahead of neighbours, home visits and group meetings; it was also more popular with young women". Similarly in Pakistan (Karlin and Ali, 1968) and in Nigeria (Ford Foundation, 1972) also it was found that radio was the prime source of family planning information for the largest percentage of people. From study conducted on radio in 22 countries, Sweeney (1977) concluded as follows :- "Radio is a first source of information according to studies carried out in Korea, Taiwan, Kenya, Honduras and Iran. However, a Columbian study identifies it as only a second source of information". Further, he noticed that radio has increased the contraceptive acceptance in Columbia, Costa Rica and Dominican Republic.

A number of studies have been conducted in India involving several media used in combination in relation to family planning. A few studies conducted in sixties (Sahawney and Langoo, 1969; Chandrasekaran and Baberto, 1963), reported that radio and newspaper hardly played any role in informing people about family planning. Similarly, a rather insignificant role of newspaper and other mass media in disseminating information about family planning was reported by Chandrasekaran and Kuder (1965) in their study of family planning clinics in Bombay. On the contrary, Dubey (1967) and Vasa (1967) found that the newspapers are a major source of information about family planning. This may be for the reason that these studies were conducted among the urban population and therefore represent the pace of change in typical urban metropolitan population.

Researches pertaining to films reflect an unusual trend. Strangely enough when the policy on films, and nature and content of films changed considerably from early to late sixties and thereupon to early seventies; there are practically no studies on films in recent times. Regarding posters, the impact of four selected pictures on family planning shown to rural women was investigated by Bhargava (1968) wherein the results indicated that in a comparison of mothers-in-law and daughters-in-law, 40 per cent of the latter had learnt about family planning through posters, while the mothers-in-law had come to know more through interpersonal source of communication.

The impact of radio as a source of disseminating family planning information was meagerly investigated and whatever data was generated under this showed somewhat contradictory results. At least three studies, Chandrasekaran and Kuder (1965), Dubey (1967), Indian Institute of Public Opinion (1967) reported radio as a poor or insignificant source for disseminating information about family planning. However, Bhende (1968) in her study on the impact of a radio-broadcast of IUD used, through a before-after survey found that only 28 per cent of the sample heard the broadcast and some of the reasons for not hearing the radio broadcast were related to the unsuitability of the time of broadcasting which usually clash with the peak hours of household work. Patel (1968) studied the impact of two radio broadcasts in family planning among 181 couples of a village in Ahmedabad and found that 25 to 50 per cent of the sample had heard the two broadcasts on family planning and each listener on an average, reported discussing it with at least six persons. However, both of these studies highlighted the usefulness of providing family planning information through the more popular programmes like Vividh Bharati, Radio Ceylon, etc.

As it is evident from the review done hitherto, there are no large scale studies on the impact of mass media on rural populations. Most of the studies are concentrated on urban populations. The only large-scale efforts made in this direction was the attempt made by the Operations Research Group (1972) who investigated this problem on a large-scale at national level. Mukherjee (1976) has synthesized the information contained in the ORG report which clearly projects the poor impact of mass media in the rural areas where it is needed most. Thus, from the existing findings it may be safely concluded that in family planning communication, through interpersonal as well as mass media, spouses play a significant role in the adoption of contraception. Hence due coverage of these variables is given in the present study.

Nevertheless most of the studies did not make any efforts to study the rightful programme variables and their acceptability. In fact such variables deserve highest priority because they are manipulable. Although incentive as a programme variable existed in the Indian family planning programme, only negligible attempt has been made in this direction. Even transport and communication do not find a place under the existing literature. Therefore, the present study gave highest importance to such of these variables, which deserve more importance in the present context.

Although value of children has been extensively used under fertility studies, it has not been used in most of the earlier studies on family planning. Hence it is an innovation in this study. Since this study is an urban oriented one, due importance is given to status of women and their modernisation as independent variables. Even these variables have not been considered in any of the earlier studies on family planning, though in recent times they have been considered under fertility studies in India (Mahadevan, 1986). Unlike the earlier studies, here we have evolved a few indexes to make wider generation of certain key variables, which have several dimensions. This approach is also innovative in the present study. Considering all these aspects the present study could make definite progress and innovations to explain maximum determinants of contraceptive behaviour. Above all these, the population studied, viz., Madras City, and particularly the Slum Dwellers form a very high priority group, since no such worthwhile study was conducted hitherto among them.

CHAPTER 2

METHODOLOGY

This chapter on methodology outlines the procedures followed for the overall execution of the present retrospective empirical study conducted in the city of Madras during 1987 period. In addition to information from the present survey, secondary data were also used for providing an overview of the demographic and family planning profile of the city of Madras in a historical perspective. It is based on a pioneering attempt made in the filed of determinants of acceptance and non-acceptance of contraception among the slum population of the city. Since, the slum dwellers in this city constitute a large population spread over an extensive geographical region across the length and breadth of the city, a sample of them have been drawn for the present study. The pages that follow discuss the objectives of the study, sample frame and size, schedule, data collection process, development of indexes, methods of analysis and finalisation of tables for different chapters, statistics used for testing the findings and so on.

Objectives of the Study

The major objectives of the study are focussed on the determinants of acceptance and non-acceptance of family planning by women of the slum population. They are as follows :

1. to study the level of acceptance and non-acceptance of family planning by different segment of slum population in the city of Madras ;
2. to study specifically certain major urban and socio-economic characteristics of the eligible couples ;
3. to study the importance of modernisation variables, status of women and their influence on contraceptive behaviour ;
4. to study the demographic factors, effectiveness of acceptors and their influence among slum population ;

5. to study the role of communication variables in contraceptive behaviour ; and
6. to study different health services (programme factors), their utilisation and their influence on adoption of contraception.

Conceptual Model

Though the number of researches conducted in the field of population studies are many and the publications, so far, available in this field are enormous, very little effort has been made to conceptualise the different determinants of contraceptive behaviour. Normally in several studies scholars depend on the analytical framework and conceptual models of fertility for applying to family planning research. Since the dependent variable of contraceptive behaviour includes a dichotomy of acceptance and non-acceptance of contraception and their determinants in toto are not the same for the fertility behaviour, separate conceptual model for this subject (family planning) is necessary. Unfortunately not many suitable models are available for this purpose now. However, the one developed by Mahadevan (1984) is the only one available in India which is very appropriate for this study. Hence, for the present study his model is adopted.

He has analytically shown the importance of different sets of factors, *viz.*, characteristics of the clients, communication variables, change agents, programme factors, etc. These were considered suitable in the present study. The dependent variable is dichotomised into adopters and non-adopters. Though number of living children was originally used as a control variable, it was deleted later on seeing its unsuitability. All other factors have been treated as independent variables for the present study.

Hypothesis

The following hypothesis focusing on the background of the respondents, communication, programme components and change agents have been considered on the basis of the conceptual model followed in this study. The determinants of contraception have been rarely conceptualised in the earlier studies. However, only one suitable conceptual model on decision-making on acceptance or non-acceptance of contraception has been contributed by Mahadevan in India (1974), which was adopted for this study, in view of its suitability for the present population.

A few specific hypothesis have been listed out here and a few more can be seen under different chapters of this thesis.

1. Socio-economic status of the slum population as a whole, is very low. Extensive illiteracy of the population deters the acceptance of contraception among this population. Though considerable occupational mobility exists among them, the family income continues to be generally low. Since socio-economic status factors are generally very low, they together act as a major barrier to acceptance of contraception in this slum population.
2. Generally social status of women also remains at a very low level, in view of the poor education and low level of modernisation of women. Hence it does not have much influence in the acceptance of contraception. This factor is measured by developing an index on status of women.
3. Though the population belongs to the urban areas and is exposed to several urban amenities of life, the general level of modernisation of this population is expected to be very low. Consequently it is not expected to influence the acceptance rate of contraception significantly. It is measured by developing an index on modernisation.
4. Value of children and particularly son preference is expected to be very great among the slum population. Hence, it is expected to determine the contraceptive behaviour adversely in this population. It is measured taking into account the number of living sons in relation to contraceptive behaviour. Further, opinion on value of children has also been considered.
5. Greater proportion of women who married early (15-17) and have long duration of married life accepted contraception because of the economic difficulty resulting out of their high fertility.
6. Monetary incentives given to the couple significantly increased their acceptance of contraception irrespective of other factors since this population belongs to very low strata of society.
7. The rate of acceptance of contraception significantly increases with the provision of acceptable pattern of health services in an accessible manner. For studying this factor

the transport conveyance and satisfaction of service facilities etc., were together considered by preparing an index on service acceptability.

8. Influence of mass media favourably and significantly promotes acceptance of contraception.
9. Satisfied adopters constitute the most effective sources of interpersonal channel of communication and their influence significantly increases the rate of adoption of contraception among the slum population.

Schedule and Indexes

Schedule

An elaborate schedule was developed for the data collection. The schedule broadly consists of twelve parts. The first part dealt will general socio-economic variables, vital events, family size and composition, cultural factors, husband-wife communication, modernisation, value of children, programme variables, service acceptability factors, incentives, family planning communication and contraceptive behaviour.

Indexes

(i) *Autonomy in Decision-making (Index)* : For constructing the overall female autonomy index in decision-making, data were collected from the respondents (wives) for the following individual major items of decision-making *viz.*, freedom enjoyed for going to shops, clubs, films, job seeking, their own future education, spending money and other day to day general familial activities. All the trichotomised respondents for each of these items, were given scores *viz.*, score 1 was assigned to those respondents who mentioned not having freedom to make decisions in these areas and score 2 was given to those answers who stated as 'enjoying partial occasional autonomy for attending to these activities and score 3 was given to those who really enjoyed full autonomy in their decision-making patterns. After assigning the scores for each of these items, these scores were pooled together for each of the respondents of the present study. The total score value was graded and classified into low, medium and high autonomous (status) categories. The minimum total of this index is 7 (since there are seven items) and the maximum score is 21. Based on these overall pooled scores, the respondents were grouped into three categories *viz.*, low status of female autonomy (scores

7-11), moderate status (12-16) and high status (17-21). This trichotomously classified index on autonomy in decision-making was cross tabulated with the contraceptive behaviour. Since autonomy of women forms a good indicator of status of women it was adopted here.

(ii) *Women's Roles (Index)* : For preparing the women's role index, all the respondents of this study were asked to state whether they are performing some of the traditional as well as new activities in their respective families. The traditional activities considered are : household work, child rearing, care of husband and other such familial activities. The new activities (roles) are : work outside home, social service, membership of voluntary associations and such other activities. A score of one has been assigned to the responses, when the respondents are performing mostly traditional activities, whereas score of two has been given if the respondents are performing mixed roles. After assigning scores along these lines, all the scores of these activities (roles) were added together separately for each respondent. These total scores form the women's roles index. The minimum and maximum scores of this index are 7 and 15 respectively. Based on this total scores, all the respondents were grouped in the three groups, *viz.*, traditional roles (score 7-9), moderate (those performing moderate number of roles (10-12), and high (those performing most of the listed roles (13+7).

(iii) *Overall Son Preference* : In order to assess respondent's overall preference for sons they were asked to state why they are very much particular to have more than one son. The possible reasons were read out to them in one after the terms of other and their views sought. These are to : assure the survival chances of one son at least; avoid risk in getting old age security, company for solitary son; have more power for defending, and other reasons. Positive responses (Yes) were assigned with a score of two. After getting the responses for all, these items were allotted with a score of one and the negative responses (No). These scores of all the six statements were pooled together for each of the respondents, which were treated as the index of respondent's overall preference for sons. According to these pooled scores, respondents have been categorised into three groups, *viz.*, respondents who have low level of son preference (scores 6-7), moderate preference for sons (8-9) and high preference for sons (10-12). This trichotomised value index was cross tabulated with the contraceptive behaviour in order to know the influence of this factor on acceptance and non-acceptance of contraception.

(iv) *Index on Satisfaction of Service Facilities* : To understand the overall health and family planning service facilities provided by the family planning programme personnel to the respondents, they were asked to mention their opinions on the following questions : (a) do the respondents have any objection to the family planning services offered by the nearest centre ; (b) are the staff members offering cafeteria approach in allowing them to choose family planning methods ; (c) whether they are satisfied with the overall services rendered by staff in respect of health aspects and family planning aspects; and (d) do the respondents consult staff for family planning and so on. A score of one is given for the negative responses, whereas a score of two is assigned to the positive responses. Afterwards these scores of all the five questions were added together for the individual respondents, which constitute the index of service facilities. Based on these indexes the respondents were categorised into three groups, *viz*., low level of satisfaction with the service facilities (scores 5-6), medium level of satisfaction (7-8) and high level of satisfaction of service facilities (9-10). This trichotomised and graded score was used to assess the influence of satisfaction on service facilities on acceptance and non-acceptance of contraceptive behaviour.

Sample Frame and Size

For the selection of sample, a random sampling procedure was adopted. At the first instance all the wards of the city of Madras have been listed out. Since, effective family planning programme is in vogue only in 99 wards, they alone were considered for the present study. It was decided on the basis of availability of family planning clinics and availability of government and voluntary agencies for the promotion of family planning programme. For representing voluntary agencies, availability of at least one agency each, like the women voluntary services, adult education centres, etc., were considered. Further, it was ensured that slum population should be available in the ward under consideration in sufficient numbers. In such wards the slum population varied from 500 to 3,000. The total slum population in all these wards put together was 8,77,263. It is out of a total population of 32,76,622 of the Madras city as a whole. Hence, the slum population comprises slightly over one-fourth of the total city population, which is the universe of the study. A list of slum population from 99 wards has

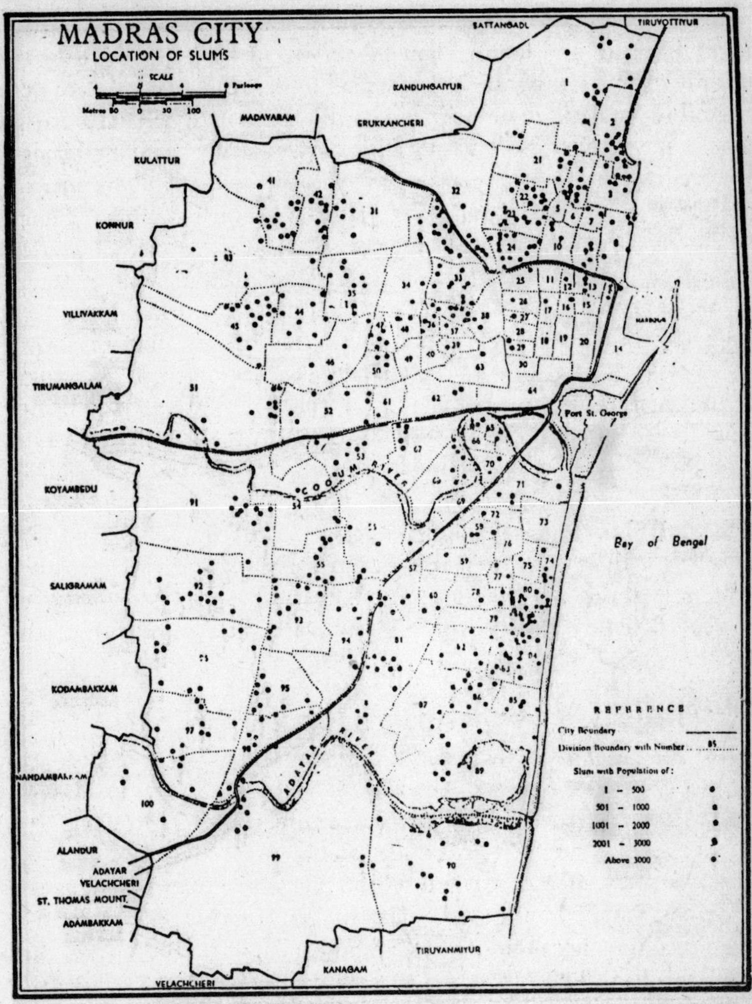
MADRAS CITY
LOCATION OF SLUMS
SCALE
Metres
SATTANGADU
TIRUVOTTIYUR
KANDUNGAIYUR
MADAVARAM
ERUKKANCHERI
KULATTUR
KONNUR
VILLIVAKKAM
TIRUMANGALAM
KOYAMBEDU
SALIGRAMAM
KODAMBAKKAM
NANDAMBAKKAM
ALANDUR
ADAYAR
VELACHCHERI
ST. THOMAS MOUNT
ADAMBAKKAM
VELACHCHERI
KANAGAM
TIRUVANMIYUR
HARBOUR
Fort St. George
COOUM RIVER
ADAYAR RIVER
Bay of Bengal
REFERENCE
City Boundary
Division Boundary with Number
Slums with Population of :
1 – 500
501 – 1000
1001 – 2000
2001 – 3000
Above 3000

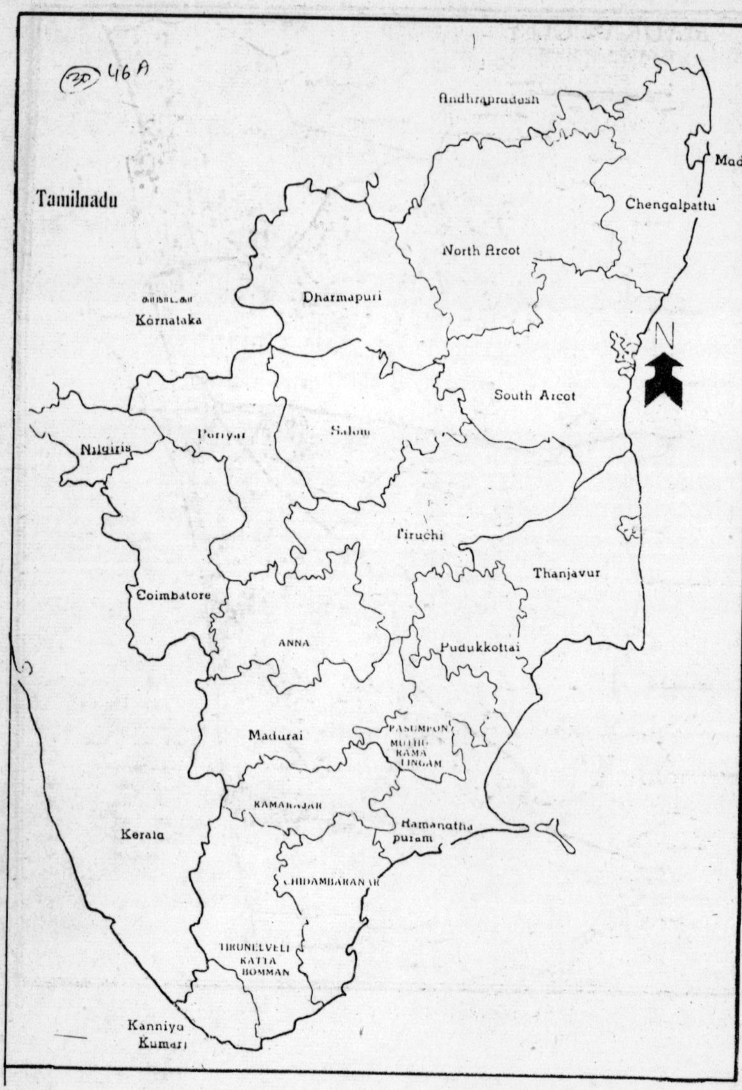
Tamilnadu
Andhrapradesh
Madras
Chengalpattu
North Arcot
Dharmapuri
Karnataka
South Arcot
N
Nilgiris
Periyar
Salem
Tiruchi
Thanjavur
Coimbatore
ANNA
Pudukkottai
Madurai
PASUMPON MUTHU RAMA LINGAM
KAMARAJAR
Ramanatha puram
Kerala
CHIDAMBARANAR
TIRUNELVELI KATTA BOMMAN
Kanniya Kumari

been prepared. It classified the slum dwellers into two strata, *viz*., adopters and non-adopters of contraception. Out of this list an equal sample of 300 current adopters and non-adopters of contraception have been separately selected at random. Thus, 600 eligible couples from an equal number of families who belong to all the 99 wards of the entire Madras constitute the total sample size of the present study. However, eligible women alone form the respondents of the study.

Interview Process

With the help of newly prepared schedule, the women were interviewed. The data collection was completed in a period of 4 months' time. The time chosen for the interview was between 6.30 A.M. to 9.30 A.M. and in the afternoon from 5 P.M. to 7 P.M. The timings were chosen very carefully to see the availability of the respondents as the women go daily to fetch water due to the water scarcity that prevailed in the city at that time. A good rapport was made with the slum dwellers by organising Health Camps before starting this survey and by introducing innovative schemes through voluntary agencies. Hence, the respondents were highly co-operative in giving the information needed for the present study.

Data Analysis

The data analysis was carried out using computer facility. A multivariate step-wise regression analysis technique was used to sharpen the understanding of the influence of different independent variables on contraceptive behaviour. X^2 (Chi-square) test was adopted for testing the association between various independent variables and contraceptive behaviour. Even in some of the frequency tables, though frequency in some cells is less than 5, X^2-test was conducted as it was justified by Ostle (1966).

[illegible]

[illegible]

[illegible]

[illegible]

[illegible]

[illegible]

CHAPTER 3

MADRAS CITY AND THE SLUM

Madras city is one of the four mega cities in India along with Bombay, Delhi and Calcutta. It is one of the ten major cities with ten million and more population according to 1981 census. The city of Madras is located on the coast line of Bay of Bengal in the Tamil Nadu state of India. It is the capital of Tamil Nadu state and forms the biggest industrial centre not only in this state but also in the Southern region of India. It was established in July 22nd, 1439 by the British Government (East India Company) and the original name of the city as Chennai Pattanam was named after Mr. Fattor Francisday who sighted the small fishing land. The city is spread over 173 sq. kms. area and has a population of 32,76,622 according to 1981 Census. Though the city has several unique features and is bestowed with several facilities, it suffers from the perennial problem of population growth particularly in the slum areas. The slum population of Madras city by 1981 constitutes 8,77,263 inhabited in 1,700 settlements. Despite the massive efforts towards slum clearance which were made by the successive governments during the last two decades, the menace of growth of slums continues unabatedly, affecting the quality of life of population in terms of pollution, environmental sanitation, health, transport and all other amenities of life. The deterioration in all-round quality of life is effected on a continuous basis with the addition of additional growth of slum population resulting from migration of people from rural areas to cities in search of jobs and more so by the rapid increase in fertility of the slum dwellers in particular. Despite the efforts so far made to curb the fertility of slum dwellers, they continue to proliferate in a big way. In the context of existing high fertility of slum dwellers in Madras city, it was decided to study them and their determinants of family planning behaviour, which is an innovative and high priority area of research now. Hence, this problem was chosen for the present thesis.

It is generally agreed that slum is not only a slum on the beauty of the city, but also reflects low living conditions of the majority of the working population. In order to undertake measures to improve the living conditions of slum dwellers, it is necessary to understand the full implication of the growth of slums. The views of the Planning Commission are definite that slums should be removed. A number of measures have been evolved and plans formulated for eliminating slums but, it is a failure in cities like Madras, Calcutta, Bombay and Delhi where slums thrive and grow faster due to several reasons.

According to corporation records of Madras there were 306 slums in the city in 1953 and it got increased to 548 in 1961 and further to 1413 by 1976 and 1700 by 1981 (MMDA) containing 97,851 households and a population of 412,168.

The Concepts of Slum

According to Oxford Dictionary a slum has been defined as follows : "a street, alley, court, etc., situated in a crowded district of a town or city and inhabited by people of low income classes or by very poor ; or a number of these streets and courts forming a thickly populated neighbourhood of a squalid and wretched character". Another interesting definition of slum was given by the Chicago School of Sociologists. In 1920s they have made significant contribution in defining the word slum. Mr. Harrey Warren Zorbaugh has defined it as follows : "The common denominator of the slum is its submerged aspect and its detachment from the city as a whole. The slum is a break area of segregated society ; an area of extreme poverty, tenements, remshackle buildings, of eviction and evaded rents ; an area of working mothers and children of high rates of birth, infant mortality, illegitimacy and death, an area of pawn shops and second hand stores. The slum harbours many sorts of people starting from criminals to the innocents". A seminar on slum clearance held in Bombay in May, 1957, has described a slum as a chaotically occupied un-systematically developed and generally neglected area which is over populated and over crowded with ill-prepared and neglected structures. Similarly during the slum survey conducted in the Madras city corporation area in 1961, the Commissioner of Madras Corporation and his staff defined it as "A slum is taken to erring area with squated surroundings. In such areas, huts are erected in a haphazard manner without proper air, protected water supply, and drainage do not exist in these areas.

Houses are built up in close proximity not allowing free air to get in. The definition of Chicago Sociologist seems to fit in very well with the characteristics of the Madras city slum. Therefore, for the present study this definition bas been considered.

PART I

Characteristics of A Slum

In Tamil Nadu slums are generally called "Cheris" and later on referred to as "Harijan colonies" and now mentioned as slums. The slum dwellers are generally tenants. The tenancy relates only to the land. Slums are formed both on the outskirts and in the heart of the city. The major problem is the cluster of huts which covers one-eighth area of the Madras city and consists of one-fourth of the total population. The slum dwellers are not merely working class people but also come from lower middle class. The slum clearance and the MMDA of the Madras city are having a tough time to provide proper shelters for the pavement dwellers, who come under the slum dwellers. During the survey conducted in 1961, it was estimated that 6,500 families of pavement dwellers, who are mostly casual labourers and beggers constituted the slum population.

The Growth of Slums in Madras City

The first census of Madras was held in 1871. At that time it had a population of 3,97,552 and an area of 2626.82 sq. miles. By 1945 and 1946, the number of suburban towns and villages in Saidapet taluk of Chingleput district were added to the city, making its total area 49.74 sq. miles. The suburbs of Madras city have developed highly urban characteristics owing to the location of industries and its close dependence on the city. The population of the city in 1961 was 1,729,141. Thus, between 1941-1961 the city had doubled its population and has now grown to five times with a population of 8,77,263 in 1981. During 1960-61 period the corporation was divided on the basis of density of population, into 100 divisions. Presently it stands at 150 divisions with an area of 170 km.

A special housing committee was appointed after the completion of 1961 survey and thus the slum clearance board was constituted by 1967 involving voluntary agencies and dividing the city

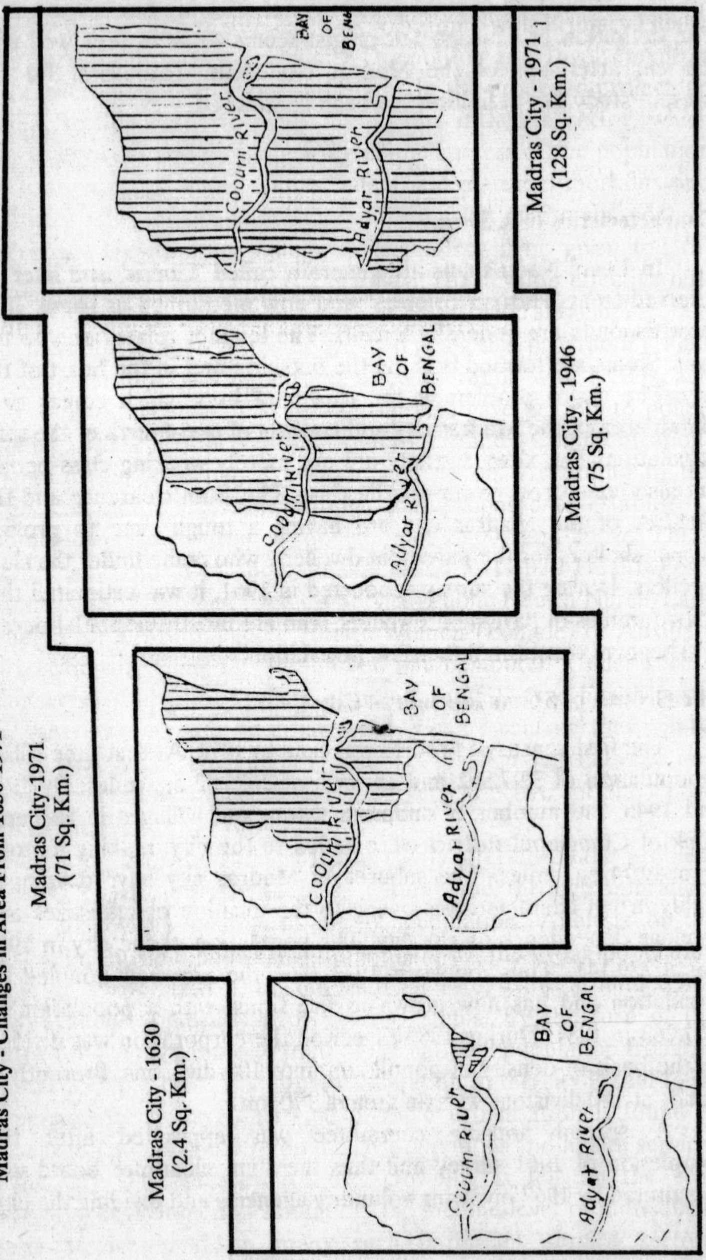

Madras City - Changes in Area From 1630-1971

Madras City - 1630 (2.4 Sq. Km.)

Madras City-1971 (71 Sq. Km.)

Madras City - 1946 (75 Sq. Km.)

Madras City - 1971 (128 Sq. Km.)

into zones like industrial zones, old residential zones, commercial zones and new residential zones. Formation of NRWT (New Residential Welfare Trust) for slum improvement brought a lot of progress and improvement in the slum area.

The religion-wise composition of population showed that the Hindus constituted 85.8 per cent, Muslims and Christians 6.3 per cent and 7.9 per cent respectively. The composition of the religious pattern of the slum population is more or less similar to the general population. The percentage of literate persons is 45.8 for males and 20.8 for females and 33.8 for both. They compare unfavourably with corresponding figures for the general population which are 69.6, 48.2 and 59.4 respectively. The above percentages are for the aggregates in age groups including infants and children.

Residence and Workspot : People's tendency to congregate in and around their places of work has been assumed to be one major reason for the development of slums. According to the household survey conducted in 1961, 77 per cent of the workers live in and around their usual place of work. It therefore follows that nearness of the workspot is one of the most important factors forcing them to live around the place of their work. Slums had been formed historically during the active movement of populations towards the city right from the Second World War onwards. Slum tenancy grew as a result of migration of the people into Madras city in search of job opportunities and thereby occupancy in slum dwellings where accommodation for living is available at a very cheap rate and close to workspot.

Efforts in the City : In 1952 Madras city constituted the committee for improving slum areas into habitable areas at a reasonable cost. So the slum improvement scheme was drafted. The corporation acquired land and started issuing pattas to the people under the scheme of "Land to the Landless". Later on, the principle of slum clearance was accepted in the 1st Five Year Plan (1956) period and thereafter till this day, government with the aid of "World Bank", has given massive assistance for the development of MMDA.

According to Table 3.1, the Madras Metropolitan Development Authority (MMDA), a major part of Madras city has been demarked under four zones as shown in the table. In these zones, together the population comprises 8,77,263 by 1981 census. But MMDA has not included the entire city of Madras under its jurisdiction. The present universe of the study includes the MMDA area only. However, the entire Madras Metropolitan area has an area of 49.4 sq. meters and 8,77,263 population according to 1981 census out of the total city population 32,76,622.

Table 3.1 : **Madras City, Slum and the Growth of Population**

Total Number of Slums	
1961	548
1971	1202
1986	1413
1989	1700
Number of Families (Zone-wise)	
(I)	15253
(II)	43539
(III)	50373
(IV)	61555
	170720
Population	
(I)	77790
(II)	226403
(III)	246828
(IV)	326242
	877263

Source : Study made by M/s Economist Group for MMDA.

Activities of Slum Clearance Board

Tamil Nadu Slum Clearance Board has been carrying out three distinct programmes in the city of Madras. This Board came into being in 1968. They have taken initially three major activities. These are : (a) slum clearance scheme ; (b) accelerated slum improvement scheme; and (c) slum improvement under World Bank Assistance.

Slum Clearance : Under this scheme huts put up in objectionable slum areas with materials like thatches, gunny, tin sheets, etc., are pulled down and multistoreyed tenements have been constructed. Slum Clearance Board builds as many number of tenements in the same area as there are eligible families so that not a single family is forced to shift to any distant place. On their initiative from 1977 to 1986, 18,362 tenements have been constructed at a cost of Rs. 1,795.51 lakhs. During 1986-87 it has proposed to construct 688 tenements at an estimated cost of Rs. 175 lakhs. Since then, they have expanded and diversified their activities. A few such activities are discussed below.

Off Site Works : According to the MUDP-II (Madras Urban Development Project II) programme, it contemplates construction of feeder drains and arterial drains to relieve the stagnation and inundation caused during times of flood in the low lying slum areas. These off site works are carried out by PWD and Madras Corporation on behalf of Slum Clearance Board. It was also envisaged to construct feeder drains by the Madras Corporation at an estimated cost of Rs. 228.40 lakhs. For this purpose already Rs. 297.76 lakhs have been deposited with the PWD for the construction of drainage works.

Poor Class Housing: Another major activity under the phase-II of this programme is the construction of houses for the poor people at a low cost. The proposal under this scheme is to provide houses to the slum families in Madras and moffussil areas, who are already provided with basic amenities. Local materials or cheap and durable building materials adopting low cost technique will be utilised for the construction of such houses. The houses will be given to slum dwellers on rental or hire purchase basis as in the case of tenemental schemes. During 1986-87, poor class housing was also extended to Madurai and Periya Nagar at a cost of Rs. 2.32 crores and 1000 such houses were completed during this period. For the future 10,562 more such houses will be constructed at a cost of Rs. 10.53 crores in other towns.

Site and Service Schemes : Another scheme taken up under MMDA is on site and service scheme which is proposed to be formulated on certain available vacant land. During 1985-86, it was proposed to take up development of 1842 plots at an estimated cost of Rs. 86.43 lakhs. Out of this, Rs. 10 lakhs was already spent during the year by obtaining loan from HUDCO, to benefit 200 families. Subsequently, 1042 families were covered at a cost of Rs. 46.69 lakhs during 1986-

87. The remaining work under this scheme was earmarked during 1987-88 period.

Cash Loan Schemes : Under this category, Slum Clearance Board has proposed the cash loan schemes for the slum area already improved under ASSS (Approved Site Serving Scheme). For this programme, HUDCO) Housing Urban Development Construction Organisation) promised 90 per cent assistance to construct houses costing Rs. 15,000 per family. Under this scheme, cash loan assistance of Rs. 8,000 will be issued to each slum family. For this scheme, proposals to a tune of Rs. 4.47 crores benefiting 5591 families have been sanctioned by HUDCO and this scheme for the year 1986-87 was already completed. More efforts under this programme are in the offing.

Community Development : With the collaboration of social welfare organisations, the Slum Clearance Board provided medical facilities, adult education and maternity and child welfare facilities in selected slum localities. A programme to generate income-supplementation has also been launched under which vocational skills training is imparted to unemployed boys and girls. So far, 4666 persons have benefited under this scheme. Slum Clearance Board helps the slum dwellers to get loans upto Rs. 200 to 2,000 from Banks at 4 per cent interest, rate to start small business also. Under this scheme, so far 2,650 families have benefited. Further, educational films stressing the importance of health, family planning and sanitation have been shown in the slum areas. Cultural programmes like Therukkoothu, Villupattu and Oranga Nadagam are performed with a view to arouse the sense of civic responsibility among them. These are some of the diversified new schemes launched by the MMDA for the benefit of slum dwellers.

PART II

Socio-Demographic Profile

A brief description of the socio-demographic parameters of Madras city is worth discussing here. The population of Madras city during 1981 was 32,76,622 of which 16,94,107 were males and 15,82,517 females. Among the total slum population in Madras city, 80 per cent belong to Hindus, followed by 13 per cent Muslims and 6.7 per cent Christians. The decadal growth rate of population during 1971-81 was 32.69. The total area of Madras city is 173 sq.

kms., and the density per sq. km. is 19 persons. The sex ratio is favourable towards males (938 females per 1000 males). On an average, there are 5 persons residing in a household. Agewise distribution of population revealed that there are 32.8 per cent in the age group of 0-14, 61.5 per cent in the age group of 15-59 and the rest 5.7 per cent are older population (60 + years).

The percentage of literacy during 1981 was 68.40. However, this rate is comparatively higher for males (75.60%) than for females (60.69%). The crude work participation rate in Madras city was 27.90. But, this rate also is much higher for males (47.92) than for females (6.46). The overall dependency ratio was 62.54 of which 53.22 belong to young dependency ratio and 9.32 old dependency ratio. The calculated singulate mean age at marriage for females was 20.6 and for males 24.8 years.

Table 3.2 : Birth and Death Rates for the Corporation of Madras City

Year	*Birth Rates*	*Death Rates*
1972	37.83	12.71
1973	36.39	12.38
1974	34.40	12.10
1975	34.28	13.08
1976	31.64	11.71
1977	32.04	11.08
1978	32.03	9.05
1979	31.07	9.05
1980	31.02	9.03
1981	31.02	9.02
1982	30.09	8.04
1983	30.97	8.63
1984	29.64	8.08
1985	28.77	7.78
1990 @	26.26	6.39
1995 @	23.93	5.26
2000 @	21.82	4.32

@ Estimated.

Source : World Bank aided population project for Madras Metropolitan Area, Project Report, Directorate of Family Welfare, Madras, 1987.

During 1985, the birth rate (CBR) recorded was 28.77 and the death rate (CDR) 7.78. The infant mortality rate for Madras city during 1984 was also much less (47). The percentage of couples protected by one or the other method of family planning was 46.3 during 1986 period. A retrospective glance at the vital events of Madras city showed that both birth and death rates started drastically declining from the year 1984 onwards. The projected decline of birth and death by 2000 A.D. are : 21.82 and 4.32 respectively, which can easily be achieved in the context of special programmes now being launched in the city under IPP-V (India Population Project V) with the assistance of World Bank (see Table 3.2).

Table 3.3 : Socio-economic Factors

Sl.No.	*Items*	*Particulars*		*Corresponding figures for Tamil Nadu*	
1.	*Religion*				
	Hindu	80.3%		89.92%	
	Muslim	13.0%		5.11%	
	Christians	6.7%		5.75%	
	Others	—		0.12%	
		100.00%		100.00%	
2.	*Age composition of the population*				
	0-4 years	14.50		11.17	
	5-9 years	13.22	39.47	11.94	34.90
	10-14 years as per survey	11.75		11.79	

3.	*Educational Status*			
	Literacy Rates :	Male	Female	Total
	Illiterate	52.8%	67.7%	59.5%
	Upto Vth Std.	21.8%	17.9%	19.9%
	VI—XII	24.7%	14.2%	19.7%
	Graduates & above	0.71%	0.2%	0.5%
		100.0	100.0	100.0

	Literacy level (1971) Census	Literacy level (1981) Census
Male	47.2%	50.3%
Female	32.3%	35.0%
Total	40.1%	46.8%

Source : Project Plan, June 1987, Directorate of Family Welfare, Madras.

PART III

Development of Family Planning

A major landmark in the development of health and family planning came into being with the establishment of Ashok Vihar. It was established originally near the former Moore market, which no longer exists. Ashok Vihar was mainly taking care of the women and children programme in the year 1930. Under its control, new branches were established in several parts of the city. Subsequently, the engineering department which was solely incharge of the sanitation, handed over the epidemic control unit to the Health Officer of the Corporation of Madras. In 1953, the different MCH (Maternal and Child Health) Centres with family welfare programme were started. In 1967 to 1974 period, the re-organisation of family welfare programme under five year plans came into being. Till recently, i.e., upto 1983 about 49 urban centres for family planning programme were established and as per this pattern (Figure-3.1) these centres started functioning with staff fully engaged in promoting family planning programme. These peripheral workers of urban family planning centres promoted family planning on the basis of cafeteria approach. However, the sterilisation operations for men or women were given preference over other methods in their motivational efforts. Corporation of Madras with the association of Maternal and Child Health Centres conducted camps in the year 1975. In these camps 6000 men below the age of 45 were sterilised. The pioneering Royapuram and Nammalwarpet camps were held with the assistance of Round Tables who gave an opportunity for the family welfare centres to improve their performance through incentives.

Family Welfare Camps

The orientation camps usually were conducted in an intensive manner twice a year and during these the adopters including motivators received incentives in cash and kind which varied from Rs. 85 to Rs. 210. Later on with the involvement of voluntary agencies several strategies were tried out. They included (1) cash incentives ; (2) special casual leave ; (3) involvement of voluntary agencies ; (4) cafeteria approach. The above method increased the acceptors rate as given in Table 3.5.

Family Planning Programme

The Corporation of Madras city started the reorganised family welfare scheme on 10th Fabruary, 1967 with one district family welfare bureau functioning at the headquarters, the Ripon Building. There are 49 urban centres functioning in the city out of which 32 are under Corporation of Madras, 4 under government hospitals and remaining 12 under voluntary agencies. Each of these centres covers a population of 50,000. All the family welfare centres under corporation of Madras are functioning in the respective child welfare centres under the leadership of one medical officer, supported by one health visitor, two auxiliary nurse midwives and one field worker (see Figure 3.1). The Commissioner of the Corporation of Madras is the administrative head and the Health Officer is the Head of the Department and the District Family Welfare Officer is in-charge of the programme. Under the Medical Officer, there are two district extension educators (One male and one female), one statistical assistant, one UDC store keeper, one typist, one driver-cum-mechanic and one office attendant (Government of India pattern).

The expenditure on the centrally sponsored family welfare scheme has been initially met by the Corporation of Madras from its funds and is being reimbursed from Government of India periodically on the production of expenditure certificate. The field staff attached to the Family Welfare Centres makes regular house visits and enlighten the eligible couples on various aspects of Family Welfare *viz.,* maternity, child care, immunisation and contraceptive methods. In all the Family Welfare Centres, IUD (Loop) insertions are done and sterilisation cases are motivated and referred to the Government hospitals and other surgical units. Individual approach, group contacts, mass education and various other methods of motivation have been used to make the people accept family welfare methods. Special intensive camps with attractive incentives and involving voluntary agencies are being done now. Under the Family Welfare Programme, emphasis is given to maternal and child health activities. Under this scheme, folic acid and other medicines are given, and immunization of pregnant women against Tetanus Toxoid is undertaken. Vitamin-A solution is also given to prevent night blindness. DPT polio and other vaccine are administered to school children through the health workers. As a result of relatively good performance under family planning Madras city won the National award for its achievement in family planning in 1973.

Highlights of the Achievements

The greater success rate of vasectomy operations achieved during 1974-75 period was mainly due to the great interest and motivational strategy adopted by the then Corporation Commissioner, Mr. T.V. Antony. The higher incentives offered to the clients at the sterilisation camps induced the males to come forward and get sterilized. During 1974-79 period, however, there was a set-back in the total achievement due to emergency proclaimed in the state due to which organised orientation camps in the year 1975-78 were not conducted and the motivational activities on male acceptors were also very low. But simultaneously the female sterilisations were carried out when the mothers got admitted for deliveries. And thus, the staff was able to motivate the mothers to undergo sterilisation which was fairly good even though the male sterilisations declined. Table 3.4 also reveals the fact that the expenditure during this period was very low when compared to previous years due to the absence of OTC's (Orientation Training Camps). In the year 1980-84 the Family Welfare Urban Centres concentrated and co-ordinated their activities with the voluntary agencies and the incentives offered were so high that female sterilisations particularly laproscopic operations in the year 1984 were relatively high. Similarly the percentage of insertions of IUD increased from 16 per cent to 26 per cent during 1985 period.

Recently under the Plan Project V the achievements as indicated in Table 3.5 show a definite improvement in the programme through the service camps. The Adult Literacy Scheme followed in 100 centres of the city slum area gave a face-lift to the programme. The women's voluntary service co-ordinated by the Family Welfare Clinics increased the attendance in urban family welfare centres and whenever OTC (Orientation Training Camp) was organised the non-adopters were motivated by educational methods and made to adopt one or the other method. In the near future, due to the innovative measures in the World Bank Project scheme the achivements are expected to be 100 per cent. Under the World Bank scheme the main emphasis would be on the integration of population control programme with primary health care services with the active involvement of NGOs (Non Governmental Organisations) like the women's voluntary service at Madras.

Figure 3.1 : Administrative Status of Urban Family Planning in Madras City

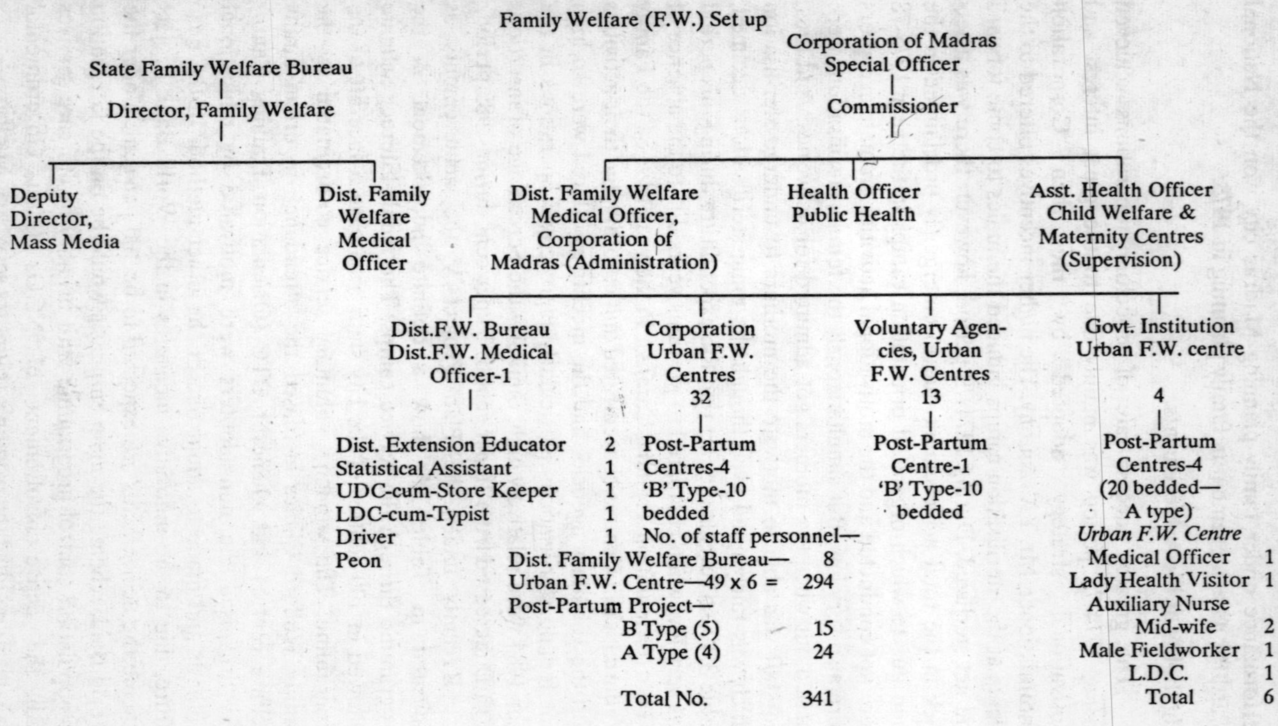

Table 3.4 : **Statement of Expenditure : District Family Planning Bureau of Madras Corporation**

Years	*Expenditure (in Lakhs of Rs.)*
1975-76	9.25
1976-77	6.42
1977-78	8.54
1978-79	9.90
1979-80	11.01
1980-81	12.43
1981-82	13.27
1982-83	17.32
1983-84	19.93
1984-85	20.36
1985-86	24.36
1986-87	69.20 @
1987-88	69.20 @
1988-89	69.20 @

@ Under Phase Plan V Project.

Expenditure

Information with regard to the expenditure on Family Welfare Programme of Madras Corporation is given in Table-3.4. On the whole the expenditure has been increasing steadily over a period of 14 years. However, it was the lowest during the year 1976-77 (Rs. 6.42 lakhs) and almost stagnant in the 1975 to 1979 period. Although the expenditure had increased progressively upto 1985-86 it was once again stagnant from 1979-82. But during the last three years the expenditure has increased almost by 3 times over and above the expenditure in the 1985-86 period (24.36 lakhs).

PART IV

Achievements of Family Planning

Table 3.5 and the graph together vividly indicate the trend in differential performance of sterilization, IUD and conventional contraceptives during the 1972 to 1988 period. All the methods did not increase uniformly over years. There was differential acceptance during different periods for one reason or the other. However, the best performance was achieved during 1973-75 period. In fact, the record level of achievements registered during 1973-74 period was largely due to the dynamism and commitment of the then Commissioner of Madras City Corporation, namely, Mr. T.V. Antony. This level of achievement could not be achieved for any method after his tenure till now. It is a pity that his successors did not display similar enthusiasm and dynamism for promoting this programme.

(a) *Sterilisations* : Data with regard to sterilisation presented in Table 3.5 suggests that in general the percentage of achievements over the targets in each year are encouraging. However, it is worth noting that the percentage of achievements in sterilisations is considerably higher during 1973-74 (290%) and 1974-75 (256.5%) period. This may be mainly due to the great interest and effective motivational strategy adopted by the then Corporation Commissioner Mr. T.V. Antony. further the enhanced incentives offered at the orientation camps attracted the males to come forward and get sterilised. In addition to these efforts, the targets laid down for sterilization during 1973-74 and 1974-75 were much less than the previous years or following years. Another peak level of achievement noticed for sterilization during the year 1981-82 was largely due to the cafeteria approach.

During 1976-77 (48%) and 1977-78 (53%) the percentages of achievements in sterilization are much less. It may be due to the adverse conditions of emergency period. The poor performance during emergency period is very unusual because, in the rest of India, in fact, a record level of family planning performance was noticed during the emergency period. Similarly, the percentage of achievement is lower during 1972-73 (52%) also because the targets laid down at that time may be very high. 1983-84 onwards the percentages of achievement in sterilization are much better. It may be because, more and more women came forward to adopt laproscopic sterilizations at the camps, which became a popular method among women.

I.U.D : The percentage of achievements with regard to IUD insertions was considerably high during most of the years under consideration. However, it was the highest during 1973-74 (315%) followed by 1975-76 (294%). However, these percentages almost started declining

Table 3.5 : **Family Welfare : Targets and Achievements—Madras City : 1972-73 to 1987-88**

Year	*Targets*				*Achievements*				*% of Achievements*			
	Sterili-sations	*IUD*	*C.C users*	*Oral pills*	*Sterili-sations*	*IUD*	*C.C. users*	*Oral pills*	*Sterili-sations*	*IUD*	*C.C. users*	*Oral pills*
1972-73	25,000	4328	7515	—	12944	5357	20358	—	51.7	123.2	270.8	—
1973-74	5,972	1798	8988	—	17314	5658	24301	—	289.9	314.6	270.6	—
1974-75	11,448	2218	46800	—	29375	5572	21402	—	256.5	251.2	45.7	—
1975-76	28,000	2134	10155	—	28655	6265	12750	—	102.3	293.5	125.5	—
1976-77	63,310	2460	11990	—	30266	6542	46465	—	47.8	265.9	387.5	—
1977-78	30,900	2460	13300	—	16304	5995	25381	—	52.8	243.7	190.8	—
1978-79	22,560	2500	8400	—	19036	5979	9392	—	84.3	239.2	111.8	—
1979-80	22,600	6500	6100	1950	20942	8002	8533	549	92.7	123.2	129.9	28.1
1980-81	20,100	2900	9500	1900	20328	7547	6982	622	101.1	260.3	73.6	32.7
1981-82	13,831	3306	10947	2206	27360	8049	3914	500	197.8	243.4	35.7	22.6
1982-83	32.200	8800	13200	2400	30663	8635	—	706	95.2	98.1	—	29.4
1983-84	45,000	13400	16600	6100	45229	13703	171	731	100.5	102.2	1.0	11.9
1984-85	46,000	30900	23200	5900	49458	24354	2054	707	106.8	78.8	8.8	11.9
1985-86	47,000	32900	25400	6200	51408	32305	3056	801	109.8	76.6	6.2	15.6
1986-87	49,000	30400	25200	6100	53444	33405	3281	902	117.6	74.2	4.2	10.4
1987-88	54,000	50200	17400	6200	54456	34501	3391	976	180.8	109.0	3.8	0.6

Source : Progress Report of Corporation Urban Family Welfare Centres.

from 1982-83 onwards due to routine operations conducted at the hospitals and other centres. It is worth studying intensively why IUD registered a poor performance from 1982 onwards.

C.C. Users : The achievements in conventional contraceptives could not be satisfactory over the years. However, the percentage of achievement for C.C. users reached the highest peak during the year 1976-77. But they are the lowest during the years 1983-84 (1.0%) onwards. Since the C.C. users registered all time increase during the emergency period, perhaps the other methods did not increase correspondingly during this period. However, the figures of C.C. users are not dependable like sterilization and IUD, when manipulation of figures by the service personnel is not very easy. In this context, it is unimaginable to see the C.C. users reaching the peak period (387.5) during 1976-77 period alone.

Oral Pills : Achievement figures for oral pills are available only from 1979-80 onwards (Table 3.5). It is because the programme is a late comer under family planning scheme. But, these figures are not statisfactory. Further, this percentage of achievement has come down considerably 1983-84 (12%) onwards. The reason was that importance to contraceptive operations was given over other methods (see Table 3.5).

Future Prospects : World Bank Project

For the improvement of the total Health Delivery and Family Planning Services in Madras City, the state and central government approached the World Bank for financial assistance. During this time, World Bank agreed to support the metropolitan programme of Madras city along with the Corporation of Bombay under Vth India Population Project. Though the full-fledged project came into being only by 1989, the preparatory work for this started right from 1986 onwards.

This project envisaged involvement of the existing service centres, namely, child welfare centres, post partum centres, urban family welfare centres and also the active involvement of over 270 voluntary organisations working throughout the city. Of course, these health centres are supposed to be reorganised on a uniform pattern with minimum worker population ratio for effective service delivery system. This project also has several short-term and long-term objectives. The project implementation organisation seen in Figure 3.2.

Figure 3.2 : India Fifth (Bombay and Madras) Population Project

Madras Project Organisation

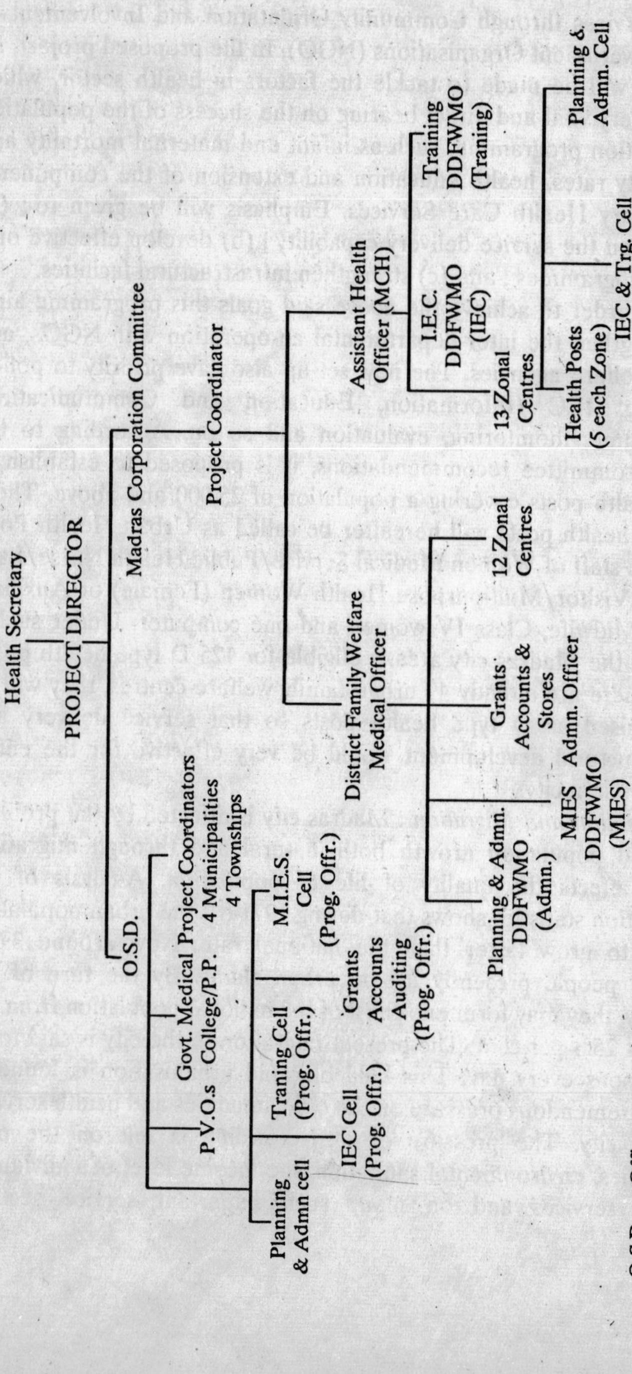

O.S.D. = Officer on special duty

Goals of the Project: The main emphasis of the programme will be to integrate population stabilisation programme with Primary Health Care Services through Community Orientation and Involvement of Non-Government Organisations (NGO). In the proposed project, an attempt will be made to tackle the factors in health sector, which have a very vital and direct bearing on the success of the population stabilization programme, such as infant and maternal mortality and morbidity rates, health education and extension of the components of Primary Health Care Services. Emphasis will be given to: (a) strengthen the service delivery capability; (b) develop effective out-reach programmes; and (c) strengthen infrastructural facilities.

In order to achieve the above said goals this programme aims to strengthen the inter-departmental co-operation with NGOs, and other welfare agencies. The new set-up also gave priority to policy, planning, IEC (Information, Education and Communication) programme, monitoring, evaluation and so on. According to the expert committee recommendations, it is proposed to establish D type health posts covering a population of 25,000 and above. These D type health posts will hereafter be called as Urban Health Posts with the staff of Women Medical Service/Public Health Nurse/Lady Health Visitor/Multipurpose Health Women (Female) or Auxiliary Nurse Midwife, Class IV women and one computer. Under such a scheme the Madras city area is eligible for 125 D type health posts. Since there are already 49 urban family welfare centres, they will be reorganised as D type health posts so that service delivery and infrastructural development would be very effective for the entire metropolitan city.

Urbanisation and Migration : Madras city is affected by the problem of rapid population growth both, natural and through migration, which affects the quality of life of population. Analysis of the population statistics shows that during 1971-81, the urban population began to grow faster than the national rate. Now around 37-40 million people presently live in urban slums. By the turn of the century, they may form one-third of the national population from the present 25.3 per cent. The present migration to the city is said to be 40 persons every day. This kind of rapid urbanisation is found to cause tremendous pressure on the civic amenities and health services in the city. The pressure of over-crowding is felt on the civic amenities, environmental sanitation, the income level of individuals, health services and on many such important service sectors.

Therefore, a timely planned project plan is welcomed to this city for improving the quality of life. Any attempt on acceptance of family planning will not be successful unless the services and other health care facilities are offered well.

The proposed plan for the 25,000 population with D type health posts envisages people's participation for effective implementation of the project by the Corporation authorities. If this project is implemented effectively there may be some improvement for the slum population in the city. But long term benefits to people in the city can be given only if suitable policy on urbanisation is adopted and translated into action. For formulating comprehensive and suitable policies, which is not there now, and for developing appropriate instrumentation, scientific data are needed. In the absence of such valuable information this study may help to a great extent.

CHAPTER 4

CULTURE AND CONTRACEPTIVE BEHAVIOUR

In this chapter, cultural factors, *viz.,* religion, caste and value of children, are discussed and they are further cross tabulated with contraceptive behaviour to know their differential influence on adopters and non-adopters of contraception among the slum dwellers of Madras city. On the basis of religious background of the respondents, they have been categorised into three distinct religious groups, *viz.,* the Hindus, Muslims and Christians.

In the study area greater proportion of the respondents (70%) belong to Hindu religion, whereas only 15 per cent each of the respondents belong to other religions, *viz.,* Islam and Christianity.

Table 4.1 : Adopters and Non-adopters of Contraception According to their Religious Background

Religion	*Adopters*	*Non-adopters*	*Total*	*%*
Hindus	59.2 (248)	40.8 (171)	100.0 (419)	69.8
Muslims	28.4 (25)	71.6 (63)	100.0 (88)	14.7
Christians	29.0 (27)	71.0 (66)	100.0 (93)	15.5
Total	50.0 (300)	50.0 (300)	100.0 (600)	100.0

X^2 = 46.720 ; Sig. at .01 level.

Religion is an important cultural factor that influences the contraceptive behaviour of the people. Several studies conducted in India and abroad have conclusively supported that the Christians, on an average adopt family planning more than the Hindus and the Muslims (Som and Sengupta, 1960 ; Sarupria, 1964 ; Kirk, 1966 ;

Presser and Bumpass, 1970; ORG, 1972; Mukherjee, 1973 ; Siddh, 1974 ; Hemalatha et al., 1977 ; Hein, 1977 ; KIFP, 1979 ; Rele and Kanitkar, 1980 ; Danda, 1984 ; Audinarayana, 1986).

Data presented in Table 4.1 supports the hypothesis that significant variations in adoption of contraception exists in this population. Hindus more than Non-Hindus adopted contraception. For instance the percentage of adopters is significantly (at 1 per cent level) higher (59%) among the Hindus, whereas the corresponding proportion is only 28 and 29 per cent respectively among the Muslims and Christians. The lower percentage of adoption among the Christians may be due to their lower socio-economic status in the slum population. And also they are being classified as Backward class in the Tamil Nadu population. Further, in order to see whether the influence of religion is uniform among all the respondents irrespective of their number of live children, analysis is being carried out accordingly and presented in Table 4.2.

Table 4.2 : Distribution of Respondents According to Religion, Living Children and Contraceptive Behaviour

Religion	*Adopters and living children*		*Non-adopters and living children*		*Total*	
	≤ 2	*3+*	*≤ 2*	*3+*	*≤ 2*	*3+*
Hindus	46.6 (95)	71.2 (153)	53.4 (109)	28.8 (62)	100.0 (204)	100.0 (215)
Muslims	24.4 (11)	32.6 (14)	75.6 (34)	67.4 (29)	100.0 (45)	100.0 (43)
Christians	11.1 (6)	53.3 (21)	88.9 (48)	46.7 (18)	100.0 (54)	100.0 (39)
Total	36.9 (112)	63.3 (188)	63.0 (191)	36.7 (109)	100.0 (303)	100.0 (297)

X^2 for ≤ 2 children 27.35, Sig. at .01 level.
3+ children = 24.39 ; Sig. at .01 level.

In general, the percentage of adopters is higher among those respondents, who have currently three or more number of children, and it is less pronounced in the case of Christians as well as among the Muslims as compared to the Hindus. Looking at the differentials in the contraceptive behaviour with two or less number of children and their religion, the Hindus are once again ahead of other two religious groups. Thus, it is confirmed beyond any doubt that Hindus in general have adopted contraception on a significant basis (significant at 1 per cent level) more than the other two religious groups irrespective of the number of living children. When we compare the level of non-adoption on the basis of religion and number of living children, significantly more proportion of respondents belonging to the Muslims and Christians opted not to adopt contraception compared to the Hindus. Between the Muslims and Christians, while more Christians with $\leq$ 2 children did not adopt it than the Muslims, opposite trend is seen with $\geq$ 3 live children between these two communities. Thus, significant variations are noticed on the basis of religion both in the case of adoption of contraception and non-adoption, irrespective of their living children.

Caste and Contraceptive Behaviour

Caste is an important cultural factor among the Hindus that affects almost all the vital decisions including adoption of family planning, as it is a composite variable within which manifest different social and cultural patterns. In general, the use of contraception is comparatively higher among the members of higher caste groups followed by the Backward caste groups and the lowest among the Scheduled caste groups. Caste and contraceptive behaviour are found to have significant association with vital events and family planning. According to some studies conducted in India Karlin, 1968 ; Shatkawat et al., 1974 ; Mahadevan, 1979, 1985 ; Ghosal and Sarkar, 1983 ; Audinarayana, 1986 ; Rao et. al.,1986, respondents who belong to the upper castes are better informed and accepted family planning methods at a higher level as compared to those of the lower castes (See Table 4.3).

In the study population, around 42 per cent of the (Hindu) respondents are scheduled castes and tribes and another 39 per cent of them belong to Backward caste like Naickers, Thuluva Vellalars and Vanniars. Another 21 per cent of them are from Forward castes like Mudaliars, Brahmins, Naidus and Pillais. However, for the present analysis only two broad caste groups, *viz.,* Backward and Forward alone is considered in view of the inadequacy of sample size of all the caste groups for their independent analysis.

Table 4.3 : Per cent Distribution of the (Hindu) Respondents Contraceptive Behaviour by their Caste

Castes	*Contraceptive Behaviour*			
	Adopters	*Non-adopters*	*Total*	*%*
SC/STs	59.4 (104)	40.6 (71)	100.0 (175)	41.8
Backward Castes	53.9 (84)	46.1 (72)	100.0 (156)	37.2
Forward Castes	68.2 (60)	31.8 (28)	100.0 (88)	21.0
Total	59.2 (248)	40.8 (171)	100.0 (419)	100.0

X^2 results showed significant at 5 per cent level.

The hypothesis confirmed here is that caste-wise variations in adoption of contraception are noticed in this population. Adoption of contraception is directly related to the status of the caste hierarchy. Data presented in Table 4.3 suggest that the percentage of adopters is significantly (.05 level) higher among the respondents of forward caste (68%) as against the SC and ST (59%) and Backward caste (54%) groups. The percentage of family planning adopters is slightly higher among the SC/ST than among the BC. It may be due to the reason that the former group is comparatively poorer in economic status which might have influenced them to adopt family planning for the sake of incentives. However, the overall findings are analogous to the findings of some of the earlier mentioned studies and thus supports the expected hypothesis.

Value of Sons and Contraceptive Behaviour

Preference for son exists more in the developing countries than in the developed regions of the world for various social, cultural and psychological reasons. Therefore, it is hypothesised that the eligible couples may adopt one or the other family planning method only after procreating their desired number of sons. Certain studies conducted in India and abroad have confirmed that value of sons showed significant influence in acceptance of contraception (Goode, 1963 ; Karlin, 1968 ; Poffenberger, 1968 ; Kaur, 1974 ; Khan, 1979 ; Rele and Kanitkar, 1980; Sivaraju, 1982 ; Reddy 1984 ; Shakilarani, 1989).

To examine the influence of the value of sons on contraception in the sample population, the contraceptive behaviour of the respondents has been analysed against the number of live sons and it is presented in Table 4.4.

Table 4.4 : Percentage Distribution of Respondents According to Preference for Sons and Family Planning Adoption Status

Preference of Sons	*Adopters*	*Non-adopters*	*Total*	*%*
No preference	60.0 (6)	40.0 (4)	100.0 (10)	1.6
One son	47.6 (126)	52.5 (139)	100.0 (265)	44.2
Two sons	51.5 (159)	48.6 (150)	100.0 (309)	51.5
Three sons & more	60.0 (9)	40.0 (7)	100.0 (16)	2.7
Total	50.0 (300)	50.0 (300)	100.0 (600)	100.0

On the whole slightly more than half of the respondents (52%) have two live sons followed by those with one live son (24%) but the number of respondents with three and more live sons is small (3%). Interestingly a negligible proportion of the respondents do not have a son at all in their family at the time of survey.

The present data confirmed the hypothesis that acceptance of contraception is positively associated with son preference by the parents. On the other hand, a negative association is noticed between non-contraception and the preference expressed for sons. The data presented in Table 4.4, suggest a steady and consistent increasing trend in the percentage of adopters with the increase in the number of sons among the respondents. For example, the percentage of adopters is only 48 per cent among those who have only one living son, which has increased to 52 and then to 60 as the number of sons increased to two and three and more respectively. Thus, the number of sons possessed by the parents is positively associated with the acceptance of contraception but it is negatively associated with the non-acceptance of contraception. By and large the preceding findings fully confirmed that the value of sons is a major determinant of acceptance of contraception for the slum population. Therefore, further details of the determinants of son preference has to be looked into in order to manipulate this factor for the promotion of family planning.

Desire for Sons and Contraceptive Behaviour

For further intensive measurement of son preference among the respondents, they have been asked to state whether they desire, and strongly desire for sons. Of those who adopted contraception, it is striking to note, that slightly less than half of the respondents (44%) have expressed strongly their preference for sons. Another 55 per cent of the adopters moderately preferred sons. Of Course, the rest of them did not show any strong preference to sons. It is further interesting to note that the largest section of respondents (56%) showed strong preference for sons, when they have not adopted contraception. Similarly, yet another 44 per cent of them also showed moderate preference for sons. These respondents would not accept contraception unless they are satisfied with optimum number of sons or alternative social security programme is provided to them (see Table 4.5).

Table 4.5 : Percentage Distribution of Respondents on the Basis of Degree of Desire for Sons and Family Planning Adoption Status

Desire for Sons	*Adopters*	*Non-adopters*	*Total*	*%*
No desire	57.9 (11)	42.1 (8)	100.0 (19)	3.2
Uncertain	70.0 (21)	30.0 (9)	100.0 (30)	5.0
Leave it to chance	53.9 (41)	46.9 (35)	100.0 (76)	12.6
Moderate desire	55.8 (86)	44.2 (68)	100.0 (154)	25.7
Strong desire	43.9 (141)	56.1 (180)	100.0 (321)	53.5
Total	50.0 (300)	50.0 (300)	100.0 (600)	100.0

Overall Importance Attached to Value of Children (Sons)

In order to assess the cumulative importance of all dimensions of the value of children (sons) that influence the respondents' contraceptive behaviour, an index has been developed (for details see the Chapter on Methodology) which classified the respondents into three groups *viz.,* sujbects with low level of value for sons, moderate preference and high preference (See Table 4.6).

Table 4.6 : Index on Value of Children Based on Score Value

Index value of children	*Adopters*	*Non-adopters*	*Total*	*%*
Low preference	48.8 (208)	51.2 (218)	100.0 (426)	71.0
Moderate preference	55.0 (73)	45.2 (60)	100.0 (133)	22.2
High preference	46.3 (19)	53.7 (22)	100.0 (41)	6.8
Total	50.0 (300)	50.0 (300)	100.0 (600)	100.0

Duration of Breastfeeding

Duration of breastfeeding may also influence the use of contraception. Generally, during the early period of lactation (about 6 to 12 months) the chances for conception will be rare and therefore, the practices of family planning may also be less. On the other hand, the rate of contraception will be higher among those couples, who have much longer duration (Say about 12 months or more) of breastfeeding, because of the chances of conception during later period of breastfeeding. Therefore, it may be hypothesised that longer the duration of breastfeeding, greater will be the chances for family planning. Data related to this aspect is provided in Table 4.7.

On the whole, slightly more than one-third of the respondents breastfed their last born children for about 7-12 months. Another 29 per cent stated that they have done it for longer periods i.e., 13-18 months and 19 months or more respectively. Interestingly, only a few of them (8%) gave breast milk for their children for a short period of hardly 6 months of feeding. Looking at the details of differentials in the adoption/non-adoption of family planning by duration of breastfeeding (Table 4.7), it is evident that the percentage of adopters is comparatively much higher (60%) among those group of respondents who breastfed their children for about a longer period (19 months or more), followed by those group of respondents who gave breast milk for a period of six months or less (50%), 13-18 months (45%), 7-12 months (45.5%). These differentials in contraceptive behaviour are statistically significant at moderate level (X^2 = 10.3794; Sig. at .05 level) and thus support the expected hypothesis in this regard. It is customary for couple not to have sex for a few months, which varies from three months to 9 months after the delivery. Therefore, they may not seriously consider to accept contraception during this period. Therefore, the existing cultural practices also influence the timing of contraception through breastfeeding.

Table 4.7: Percentage Distribution of Family Planning Status by Duration of Breastfeeding

Duration of Breastfeeding	*Adopters*	*Non-adopters*	*Total*	*%*
≤ 6 months	50.0 (24)	50.0 (24)	100.0 (48)	8.0
7-12 months	45.5 (95)	54.5 (114)	100.0 (209)	34.9
13-18 months	45.3 (78)	54.7 (94)	100.0 (172)	28.6
19+ months	60.2 (103)	39.8 (68)	100.0 (171)	28.5
Total	50.0 (300)	50.0 (300)	100.0 (600)	100.0

X^2 = 10.3794; Sig. at .05 level.

When the overall son preference was considered taking into account all the dimensions of value of sons, nearly two-thirds of the respondents gave only low preference to sons among the adopters and non-adopters. Thus, the degree of value of sons is found to be very strong among a very large segment of adopters and non-adopters. It is found to be more extensive among non-adopters than adopters. The X^2 results also supported the association between desire for sons and contraceptive behaviour (X^2 = 7.04, df. 2 sig. at 0.5 level). These findings are also concurring with the earlier studies done by Goode (1963) who pointed out the significance of son preference as a variable strongly determining the contraceptive use. He quotes a WHO study in 1950's carried out in Lodi Colony, which found that young couples, even though they favour family planning, did not use any method consistently, because they did not have the number of sons they desired.

For the present study it was hypothesised that those respondents who expressed higher preference towards value of children may be less likely to adopt one or the other method of family planning as compared to those who mentioned moderate and low preference for value of male children. Data given in Table 4.6 do not fully support this hypothesis. The degree of son(s) preference did not show any consistent differential by way of greater influence among the non-adopters, which was hypothesised in this study. Of those respondents who had low level of son preference, about 51% did not accept contraception. However, the percentage of adopters is comparatively less (46%) among those respondents who gave highest preference for value of male children as against those respondents who stated less and moderate preference towards value of male children. These differences indicate a trend in the expected direction but are not statistically significant. Generally speaking value of sons act as one of the determinants of non-acceptance of contraception among the non-adopters.

did not use any method consistently, because they did not have the number of sons they desired.

For the present study it was hypothesised that those respondents who expressed higher preference towards value of children may be less likely to adopt one or the other method of family planning as compared to those who mentioned moderate and less preference for value of male children. Data given in Table 4.6 do not fully support this hypothesis. The degree of son(s) preference did not show any significant differentiation by way of greater influence among the non-adopters, which was hypothesised in the study. Of those respondents who had low level of son preference, about [illegible] did not accept contraception. However, the percentage of adopters is comparatively less ([illegible]) among those respondents who gave highest preference for value of male children as against those respondents who stated less and moderate preference towards value of male children. These differences indicate a trend in the expected direction but are not statistically significant. Basically speaking value of sons acts as one of the determinants of non-acceptance of contraception among the non-adopters.

CHAPTER 5

SOCIO-ECONOMIC CHARACTERISTICS AND CONTRACEPTIVE BEHAVIOUR

Historically, studies carried out in many Western countries have shown that there has been strong relationship between socio-status and fertility. However, the empirical research carried out since the Indianapolis study, revealed changes in the conventional relationship between status variables and fertility. Deborah Freedman (1963) explained the reasons for this shift in the traditional relationship. According to her, "Large families were more prevalent among the poor and un-educated. Recently, these differentials have narrowed or even been reversed in some places. This change was predicated by a number of authors for two reasons : (i) as our population has become more universally educated and urbanised, knowledge of contraception is no longer limited to the higher socio-economic group, so that an effective choice of desired number of children is possible for all strata, and (ii) as our economy has lost its rural character, children have become their economic utility". During the recent past almost all developed countries started regulating their population growth to the desired level by using family planning and also through socio-economic development.

The socio-economic status variables discussed in this chapter include type of house, education of wife, education of husband and family annual income.

Type of House

Type of house is one of the important macro indicators used to measure the socio-economic status of the people. In the study area only two types of houses, namely, hut and pucca houses are noticed.

In the population as a whole, an overwhelming proportion (71%) of the slum dwellers reside in the huts and the rest (29%) live in the pucca houses provided to them by the Madras Metropolitan

Development Authority (MMDA) under the slum clearance programme. It is clear from Table 5.1 that the percentage of adopters, is

Table-5.1 : Per cent Distribution of Respondents' Contraceptive Behaviour by Type of House

Type of House	*Contraceptive Behaviour*			
	Adopters	*Non-adopters*	*Total*	*%*
Hut@	53.1 (198)	46.9 (112)	100.0 (300)	70.7
Pucca	42.6 (102)	57.4 (298)	100.0 (300)	29.3
Total	50.0 (300)	50.0 (300)	100.0 (600)	100.0

The X^2 results 5.44 and significant at 0.05 level.

@ There is not much difference between huts and semi-pucca houses. In fact most of the houses have the characteristics of huts only.

significantly (at 0.05 level) higher (53%) among those respondents who are residing in huts than those respondents residing in the pucca houses (43%). For non-adopters an exactly reverse trend is noticed contrary to what was expected. The possible reason may be that most of the respondents who are residing in huts would have been influenced by incentives and accepted contraception out of poverty. Among the adopters and non-adopters, it is observed that there is not much difference between the residents of huts and semi-pucca houses.

Education of Wife

Education of wife is one of the vital indicators of the status of women. In almost all developed countries, fertility level is very low mainly because of the high literacy rate of women. From the demographic point of view, education of women increases their age at marriage, reduces duration of fertile period of reproductive life, develops small family norm, motivates them to have longer spacing and lastly increases their participation in family planning adoption by choosing an appropriate contraceptive. The hypothesis generally have been confirmed in many studies through a positive association between education of wife and adoption of contraception.

Stycos (1970) found a positive association between the use of contraception and women's level of formal education in Latin

America. Further, he confirms that "Women with no education have had 3.3 times as many births as those with one or more years of college. If the progress were distributed evenly, over the approximately 14 years of education, it would mean that each additional year of schooling produced 0.4 fewer live births or well over one birth for every three years of schooling". Two major Indian studies (Mysore Population Study (U.N. 1961) and Khanna Study, (1971) (Wyon and Gordon, 1971)—have specifically showed that longer period of schooling for girls reduces fertility and increases their participation in decision-making for choosing family planning methods.

Majority of the slum population is either illiterate or hardly educated. In the sample slum population, a sizeable proportion (39%) of the respondents was illiterate. Another 44 per cent of them got education only upto primary level (1-5 classes). Highly educated constitute only 17 per cent, those who completed education upto secondary and above (6+ classes).

Table 5.2 : Per cent Distribution of Respondents' Contraceptive Behaviour by Educational Status

Educational Status	*Adopters*	*Non-adopters*	*Total*	*%*
Illiterates	58.3	41.7	100.0	39.2
	(137)	(98)	(235)	
Primary (1-5) classes	40.3	59.7	100.0	43.8
	(106)	(157)	(263)	
Secondary +	55.9	44.1	100.0	17.0
	(57)	(45)	(102)	
Total	50.0	50.0	100.0	100.0
	(300)	(300)	(600)	

X^2 results; 5019 and significant at .01 level.

Data presented in Table 5.2 confirms the expected hypothesis only among the respondents who are educated upto primary and secondary levels. For example, the percentage of adopters is significantly lower (40%) among those who are educated upto primary level, while it has increased to 56 per cent among those whose education is secondary level and above. However, it is striking to note that this percentage is much higher among the illiterates (58%). The reason is that the mothers were often contacted by the Health workers and animaters under adult education for orientation camps on contraception and thus they have been motivated to adopt one or the other methods of family planning.

Table 5.3 provides information about the percentage distribution of the respondent's contraceptive behaviour on account of their husbands' education. In the population as a whole around 60 per cent of the husbands have got education upto the secondary and higher secondary level. Further, another 21 per cent have attained primary education, while another 20 per cent are illiterates. In this slum population, husband are comparatively much better in their educational status as againt their wives.

Table 5.3 : Per cent Distribution of Respondents' Contraceptive Behaviour by the Educational Status of Husband

Educational level of the Husband	*Contraceptive Behaviour*		*Total*	*%*
	Adopters	*Non-adopters*		
Illiterate	60.2 (71)	39.8 (47)	100.0 (118)	19.7
Primary	56.8 (71)	43.2 (54)	100.0 (125)	20.8
Secondary	43.9 (79)	56.1 (101)	100.0 (180)	30.0
Higher Secondary+	44.6 (79)	55.4 (98)	100.0 (177)	29.5
Total	50.0 (300)	50.0 (300)	100.0 (600)	100.0

The X^2 results : 11.93 significant at .05 level.

An exact negative association is observed between the educational level of husbands and their wives' contraceptive behaviour. For instance the percentage of adopters is significantly higher among the illiterate husbands (60%) and those husbands educated upto the primary level (57%). Those husbands who are educated upto secondary and higher secondary level could influence only 44 per cent and 45 per cent of their wives respectively to accept contraception. The observed negative association is an unexpected feature which may be because most of the wives in the population though illiterate are motivated towards adoption of contraception due to pressure of poverty and attraction of incentives. This can be further seen in the subsequent chapter.

Work Status of Wives and Contraceptive Behaviour

Occupation of wife is one of the socio-economic status indicators that influence contraceptive behaviour. In India, occupational status and mobility are not high when compared to the developed countries, which may be mainly due to the low level of literacy and the slow pace of industrialization. Some of the studies have conclusively proved that working women are more inclined to adopt one or the other method of family planning than house wives. Many studies (Freedman, 1959; Johnson, 1960; Heer, 1964; Kiser et al., 1968; Ridley et al., 1969) have found a negative association between female participation in the labour force and fertility. Atleast two explanations are offered for this association. First, female participation in the labour force may delay marriage and consequently reduce fertility. A job may also demand commitments that are incompatible with, and to a certain extent alternative to marriage. Moreover, employment can be viewed by the working wife not only as a source of additional income but also as an avenue towards achieving a higher status and self fulfilment or as an escape from the burden of the house (Pohlman, 1969). Blake (1965) has suggested that women's preference for work and child-bearing may have reciprocal effects on each other. According to Weller (1977) the negative correlation between wives' employment and their cumulative family size is stronger among the whites than the non-whites. In the KIFP study (1979) the practice rates by employment status indicate that women currently working are more likely to be practicing contraception than housewives.

Table 5.4 : Per cent Distribution of the Respondents' Contraceptive Behaviour by their Work Status

Work status	*Adopters*	*Non-adopters*	*Total*	*%*
House wives	49.2 (270)	50.8 (279)	100.0 (549)	91.5
Workers	58.8 (30)	41.2 (21)	100.0 (51)	8.5
Total	50.0 (300)	50.0 (300)	100.0 (600)	100.0

In the study area an overwhelming proportion of the respondents (91.5%) comprises of house wives and the remaining negligible percentage of them (8.5%) work outside their homes either for daily wages or for salaries. The working women include house-maid, vegetable or flower vendor and construction labourers.

As hypothesised, the percentage of family planning adopters is comparatively higher among those women working (59%) outside home than among those who do not work (49%). However, these differentials in contraceptive behaviour by the work status of the respondents did not turn out to be statistically significant, which may be due to the smaller sample size of the worker. Nevertheless the trend is as expected. These findings, however, provide an indication that any effort made to enhance the status of women may directly benefit the family planning programme.

Occupation of Husband and Contraceptive Behaviour

Occupation of the husband is yet another socio-economic indicator influencing contraceptive behaviour. Most of the earlier studies proved that there exists a positive association between the upward occupational mobility of the husband and favourable contraceptive behaviour. To test this hypothesis in the present study the occupational status of the husband has been cross tabulated with the contraceptive behaviour (see Table 5.5).

Based on the similarities and dissimilarities in the individual occupation of the husbands, three major groups have been formed here, *viz.*, unskilled, skilled and personnel workers. In the study area majority of the husbands belong to the unskilled category of workers, who are mostly engaged in construction work or daily wage earners like rickshaw pullers, coolies and servants. Another sizeable proportion (28%) of the husbands were engaged in skilled work such as carpentry, plumbing and also as electricians and petty businessmen. However nearly one-fourth of the husbands are employed in government service and in the non-government service.

Table 5.5 reveals that the percentage of adopters is significantly higher (61.1%) among the unskilled category of workers than among the skilled (43%) and business (43%) categories, and as well as professional and personnel workers (38%). It goes against the hypothesis set here for observation. It may be because the status improvement in the non-traditional occupational category is not sufficient to make any behavioural change. The X^2 results also concur on similar lines. The other reason is that the slum population constitutes a mixture of lower occupational strata and also the absence of husbands during the time of family planning motivation.

Table 5.5 : Per cent Distribution of the Respondents' Contraceptive Behaviour by Occupational Status of their Husbands

Occupational status of husband	*Adopters*	*Non-adopters*	*Total*	*%*
No work	16.7 (1)	83.3 (5)	100.0 (6)	1.0
Unskilled (Carpentry, Plumbing, Electricians)	61.1 (173)	38.9 (110)	100.0 (283)	47.2
Skilled (Business, professionals)	42.5 (71)	57.5 (96)	100.0 (167)	27.8
Workers (Educated employee)	38.2 (65)	61.8 (99)	100.0 (164)	24.0
Total	50.0 (310)	50.0 (310)	100.0 (620)	100.0

The X^2 result 25.66 and significant at 01 level.

Annual Family Income and Contraceptive Behaviour

Annual family income is considered here as an important economic factor that determines the practice of family planning. A number of studies have conclusively proved that the users of family limitation methods will increase with an increase in their income level. Several of the studies (Westoff et al., 1963; Campbell, 1968; Walvekar et al., 1974; Carvajal and Gaithman, 1976) have shown positive relationship between economic status and adoption of contraception. Whelpton et al., (1966) and Rainwater (1960, 1965) reported from their studies that in the United States, the lower class people have more children than the middle and upper classes and lower class fertility appears to be high due to insufficient and ineffective use of contraception. Carvajal and Gaithman (1976) found that not only does the use of contraception tend to increase with the level of income, but also adoption of more sophisticated contraceptive techniques is more likely to occur among higher income couples. On the other hand, Srivastava (1974) inferred that the influence of income on family planning acceptance operates through the monetary incentives offered as a strategy of programme implementation. It is greater among people with lower family income. However, in Mysore Population Study (U.N. 1961) it was found that economic status positively related to the practice of family planning.

To examine this hypothesis in the present study, the information about the annual family income has been collected, and cross tabulated with the contraceptive behaviour and is presented in Table 5.6.

Table 5.6 : Per cent Distribution of the Respondents' Contraceptive Behaviour According to the Annual Family Income

Annual Family Income (in Rs.)	*Adopters*	*Non-adopters*	*Total*	*%*
≤ 3,000	38.0 (35)	62.0 (57)	100.0 (92)	15.3
3,000 - 4,000	45.7 (74)	54.3 (88)	100.0 (162)	27.0
4,000 - 5,000	61.2 (79)	38.8 (50)	100.0 (129)	21.5
5,000 - 6,000	50.0 (64)	50.0 (64)	100.0 (128)	21.3
6,000 +	54.0 (48)	46.0 (41)	100.0 (89)	14.8
Total	50.0 (300)	50.0 (300)	100.0 (600)	100.0

The X^2 result 13.60 and significant at .05 level.

In the sample slum population slightly more than one-fourth of the respondents are in the annual family income group of Rs. 3,000 - 4,000 followed by 21 per cent each who are in the income categories of Rs. 4,000 - 5,000 and Rs. 5,000 - 6,000 per annum. However, 15 per cent each of the respondents belong to the lowest (Rs. ≤ 3,000) and the highest income groups (Rs. 6,000 +).

Data presented in Table 5.6 also suggest that practice of family planning methods has by and large steadily increased with increase in the level of annual family income except in the middle income group, and thus partially confirms the earlier hypothesis in this regard. For instance the percentage of adopters is only 38 per cent among the respondents whose annual family income was ≤ Rs. 3,000 which has increased to 54 per cent among those respondents whose annual family income was Rs. 6,000 and above. More or less supporting this hypothesis, a negative association is noticed between economic status and non-contraception with a slight inconsistency noticed for one category of income. Monthly or annual family income is considered as an important economic factor that determines the practice of family planning. Generally, use of family limitation methods increases with economic status of the family (Agarwala, 1960; U.N. 1961; Sarupriya 1964; (ORG), Kaur, 1974; Khan, 1979; Bisaliahand Gowda, 1981; Government of India, 1986). Thus family income constitutes a major determinant of contraceptive behaviour.

All the socio-economic status factors also influence contraception except occupation, which shows negligible variations among the people of the slum area. They all, of course, do not uniformly support any negative or positive relationship with contraception. These inconsistencies may be due to their general poor socio-economic status. Though education and type of house do not manifest any expected direct relationship in this analysis, income and occupational mobility of wife showed an expected result of positive association with the acceptance of contraception.

CHAPTER 6

MODERNIZATION, STATUS OF WOMEN AND CONTRACEPTIVE BEHAVIOUR

Modernization : Modernization, according to Goldschneider (1971) encompasses two broad dimensions—development of social structure, and development of institutional structure. The development of institutional structure comprises changes in a set of values, attitudes and goals, personal, cultural and general ways of thinking and acting. The development of social structure comprises changes in education, wives employment and their cumulative (total) family size.

Modernization is a macro concept that encompasses several dimensions of individual, society, culture, technology, development and human behaviour. It refers to a progressive development in natural aspects of human life. Generally, modernization can be perceived in a variety of manifestations and latest behaviour patterns emanating from one, or a series of progressive changes occurring in diverse dimensions of society in general. Here, we consider the behavioural aspect alone to study modernization.

In the present study an attempt is made to know the level of modernization of the respondents and its influence on their family planning adoption status by asking their opinions and experiences about various aspects of day to day life. The traits of modernization considered here include several dimensions since this concept is a multidimensional one. They are : religious tolerance and secularism, views on higher age at marriage (18+ years) for girls, belief in fortune telling, type of treatment preferred for children, listening to radio. These dimensions of modernization have been selected after considering a dozen of them since these alone were found to be sensitive. It is assumed that those people who express modern views about these aspects are more likely to adopt one or the other methods of family planning than those who hold traditional opinion on these aspects.

Under this chapter a few dimensions of individual modernity roles of women and their autonomy have been considered to explain the variation in contraceptive behaviour. Since modernity is affected by diverse factors, they have been individually analysed here against contraceptive behaviour. However, two indices have been considered in the case of autonomy and roles of women because items can be conveniently pooled into an index using an equal interval scoring pattern. In fact, autonomy of women forms yet another dimension of modernization though it is a variable by itself. The first part deals with exclusive modernization and the second part refers to autonomy and roles of women.

Religious Life and Modernity

Religion plays an important role in influencing the behaviour of people in India. In the present study, the religiosity of the respondents is measured on the basis of their views on whether or not they will consider that there are valuable teachings in other religions like in their own religion. Those respondents who consider that there are valuable teachings in other religions like in their own have been categorised as relatively modern women. The others are categorised as less modern and traditional. From Table 6.1 it is clear that a greater proportion of respondents (86%) is fairly modern in their religious life and the rest of them are 'more religious' (traditional). For the present study it has been hypothesised that the rate of family planning adoption will be higher among those respondents, who are modern in their religious life than those who are highly religious (fundamentalist).

Results from Table 6.1 suprisingly confirm that a greater proportion of adopters (72%) are found among those respondents, who are more religious (traditional) as compared to those who are relatively modern. The X^2 results also revealed that these differentials are statistically highly significant (X^2 = 18.764; sig. at .01 level). This type of trend may be because modernization does not show any sensitivity because of the low level of modernization generally noticed among slum dwellers. Further, the economic backwardness also might distort the trend because they may be influenced by incentives for adoption of contraception.

Opinion About the Age at Marriage

Most of the traditional people marry off their girls at early ages. But, with the influence of modernization now-a-days people

Table 6.1 : A few Dimensions of Modernization and the Adoption Status of Contraception

Dimensions of Modernization	*Adopters*	*Non-adopters*	*Total*	*%*
(i) *Religiosity*				
More religous	71.8	28.2	100.0	14.2
	(61)	(24)	(85)	
Relatively modern	46.4	53.6	100.0	85.8
	(239)	(276)	(515)	
			X^2 = 18.764; Sig. at .01 level.	
(ii) *Opinion about higher age at marriage (after 18 years for girls)*				
Disagree	25.0	75.0	100.0	4.0
	(6)	(18)	(24)	
Agree	51.0	49.0	100.0	96.0
	(294)	(282)	(576)	
			(X^2 = 6.750; Sig. at .01 level.	
(iii) *Opinion on belief in fortune telling*				
Agree	46.3	53.7	100.0	61.5
	(171)	(198)	(369)	
Disagree	55.8	44.2	100.0	38.5
	(129)	(102)	(231)	
			X^2 = 5.132; Sig. at .05 level.	
(iv) *Type of Treatment given to children*				
Allopathic (DOC)	51.0	49.0	100.0	95.7
	(293)	(281)	(574)	
Others	26.9	73.1	100.0	4.3
	(7)	(19)	(26)	
			X^2 = 5.784; Sig. at .05 level.	
(v) *Listening to Radio programmes*				
Not/rarely	60.5	39.5	100.0	28.7
	(104)	(68)	(172)	
Often	45.8	54.2	100.0	71.3
	(196)	(232)	(428)	
			X^2 = 10.562; Sig. at .01 level.	
Total	50.0	50.0	100.0	100.0
	(300)	(300)	(600)	

are preferring late marriage for their children, especially of their daughters (girls). With this assumption in view, the respondents of present study have been asked to give their opinions with regard to the higher age at marriage (after 18+ years) for girls. Those respondents who agreed that higher age at marriage for girls will be good are treated here as modern, whereas those who disagreed with it are considered as traditional. In the study area, an overwhelming proportion (96%) of the respondents agreed to the idea of late age at marriage for girls and only a negligible 4 per cent of them did not agree to this (see Table 6.1) idea.

Here, it has been hypothesised that the respondents who are willing for late marriage of girls would be more readily adopting family planning methods compared to the others, who did not agree to it. A glance at Table 6.1 confirmed this hypothesis. The percentage of adopters of family planning is significantly higher (51.0) among those respondents who agreed for the higher marriage age for girls (after 18 years) than among those who did not agree to a higher age at marriage (25%). A reverse trend is noticed in the case of non-adopters. Further, these differentials in family planning adoption status are also found statistically significant ($X^2 = 6.750$; Sig. at .01 level).

Belief in Fortune Telling

Generally, traditional people have greater belief in fortune telling and may often use it for personal needs. However, due to higher education and modernization in particular, people have changed their belief in this regard and therefore, we assume that modernised people in the recent past may not be influenced by fortune telling. Therefore, in the present study, it has been hypothesised that the respondents who have belief in fortune telling are less likely to adopt family planning methods as compared to those respondents who do not bother about it.

In the study area, slightly more than three-fifths of the respondents (61.5%) expressed that they believe in fortune telling, whereas the rest of them (38.5%) said that they do not have belief in fortune telling. This shows clearly that majority of the respondents in the slum area of Madras city have a traditional opinion regarding their future.

The overall findings of the present study (Table 6.1) reveal that the percentage of adopters is relatively less among those who have belief in fortune telling (46%) than those who do not have belief about it (56%). The X^2 results also turned out to be moderately significant (X^2 = 5.132, Sig. at 0.05 level) between the belief and no belief in fortune telling groups and their family planning adoption status. The findings thus confirmed that traditional belief in fortune telling deters the acceptance of family planning. On the other hand decline of traditional belief in fortune telling facilitates the clients to accepts contraception. Hence, it is fairly certain that modern attitude towards future life and its predictability makes people favour contraception.

Type of Treatment giving to Children

In general, people who have modern way of life prefer to treat themselves as well as their children with allopathic and homoeopathic physicians (doctors), when they fall ill. But traditional people may go for treatment to various types of other indigeneous physicians or do self medication. The respondents of the present study have been asked to state the actual type of treatment they usually followed for their children when they fell ill during the recent times. It is to assess their relative traditional/modern way of life in the field of medication. For the present study, it has been hypothesised that the proportion of adopters will be greater among those respondents who have taken treatment for their children from allopathic/ homoeopathic physicians, whereas it will be less among those who have taken other types of treatment.

The generalisation that emerges out of this study suggests that the percentage of adopters is comparatively higher (51%) among those respondents who have taken treatment for their children from allopathic doctors than among those who treated their children with the help of indigeneous medicine/self medicine (27%). The X^2 results also confirmed that these differences are moderately significant (X^2 = 5.784; Sig. at .05 level) and thus the preceding hypothesis has been proved by this findings.

Listening to Radio Programmes

Listening to radio programmes is considered to be a good modern habit. Listening to radio everyday to hear about various aspects of day to day life and news (national and regional) may change the traditional behaviour of the people leading to modernization. Information about the different aspects of family welfare programme will be heard by those people who often listen to radio programmes, which may motivate them to adopt one or the other methods of family planning. Therefore, in the present study it is hypothesised that the percentage of adopters will be higher among those respondents who listen to radio often as compared to those respondents who listen to it rarely or not at all.

On the whole, in the study area, 71 per cent of them are listening to radio 'often' and the rest, 29 per cent of them listen to radio rarely or not at all. However, from Table 6.1 it may be noticed that, the percentage of adopters is much higher (60.5%) among those respondents who listen to radio rarely, not at all, whereas adoption of contraception is less (46%) among those who often listen to radio programmes. This trend is exactly opposite to the hypothesis postulated here. Therefore, the findings do not support this particular hypothesis. It may be because poor people who do not have radio and cannot listen to it might have adopted family planning with the influences of incentives and other powerful factors.

Status of Women

Status of women plays a crucial role in depressing the fertility and therefore, may increase the adoption of family planning. But empirically, measuring status of women is a difficult and complex endeavour. However, in this section an attempt is made to examine some selected dimensions of status of women and their influence on the adoption/non-adoption of family planning. The dimensions of status of women considered here form indices based on certain interrelated aspects. They are : Autonomy in decision-making index, roles of women index, and roles indexed on family planning adoption status.

Autonomy in Decision-making (Index)

Generally, major and final decisions in day-to-day life matters are taken by male spouses and thus female spouses will be neglected in this regard. But due to higher education, modernization and social change, females in the recent past are usually involved in making certain decisions. This develops female autonomy, which in turn leads to higher status for women and an increase in the adoption of family planning, leading to reduction in family size. In the light of this, the respondents (females) of the present study have been asked to state whether they used to make independent decisions with regard to the following items : shopping, going to club, films, job seeking, their own future education, spending money and other day-to-day familial activities. Based on the responses received for these items, an index on female autonomy has been prepared (for details see Methodology chapter) and cross-tabulated with their family planning adoption status. All the respondents have been classified into low status, moderate status and high status groups on the basis of their index of female autonomy (see Table 6.2). For the present study, it is hypothesised that the adoption of family planning will increase with an increase in the status of women as reflected by female autonomy.

From Table 6.2 it is evident that slightly more than half of the respondents (55%) in the study area have moderate status, whereas 42 per cent of them have higher status. Interestingly only 3 per cent of the respondents have very low autonomy. An analysis of family planning status by autonomy index (Table 6.2) reveals that the

Table 6.2 : Index of Autonomy of Women

Index of Autonomy (Scores)	*Adopters*	*Non-adopters*	*Total*	
7 - 11	42.1 (8)	57.9 (11)	100.0 (19)	3.2
12 - 16	52.7 (173)	47.3 (155)	100.0 (328)	54.7
17 - 21	47.0 (119)	53.0 (134)	100.0 (253)	42.1
Total	50.0 (300)	50.0 (300)	100.0 (600)	100.0

X^2 = 2.353; Not significant.

percentage of adopters is lower (42%) when the women enjoy less autonomy, whereas it has increased to a higher level of 53 per cent, when their autonomy is at moderate level. However, a slight decline is noticed for women with higher level of autonomy (47%) which is unexpected. Thus the overall findings exhibited a somewhat positive curvelinear relationship between the index of female autonomy and adoption of family planning.

Roles of Women (Index)

In India, women are expected to perform certain traditional roles, *viz.*, household work, child-rearing, caring for their husband and extending love and affection towards all the member of the family. However, due to higher education and modernization women now-a-days perform certain new roles like spending time in educating their children, working outside home (either in agricultural or non-agricultural sector) etc. Therefore, adoption of more and more new roles and particularly of modern ones outside their home will reflect better status in society. Naturally, as women gain a better status in the family and society they will think and act in the right direction. With this background, in the present study respondents have been asked whether they perform the following traditional and new roles, *viz.*, household work, child rearing, care of husband, others, work outside home, social service and other new activities. Based on their answer to each role an index has been prepared (see Methodology chapter) to decide their overall status. Hence, it has been hypothesised that the extent of practice of contraception will increase with the diversification and modernization of their roles in society.

Table 6.3 : Roles Index and Family Planning Adoption Status

Roles Index	*Adopters*	*Non-adopters*	*Total*	*%*
7 - 9	58.0 (40)	42.0 (29)	100.0 (69)	11.5
10 - 12	49.1 (255)	50.9 (264)	100.0 (519)	86.5
13 +	41.7 (5)	58.3 (7)	100.0 (12)	2.0
Total	50.0 (300)	50.0 (300)	100.0 (600)	100.0

From Table 6.3 it is clear that a greater proportion of the respondents (86.5%) have moderate number of roles (index) with traditional and certain modern ones. Whereas 11.5 per cent of them have mostly traditional limited roles. As expected, for this slum, very negligible number of dwellers play modern roles in their day-to-day life (2%). As many as 58% of women, who perform mainly traditional roles in their day-to-day life, adopted contraception. It might be because, these roles give them more problems and difficulties with high fertility. When women assume more and more new roles, the opportunity cost may also go up, leading to acceptance of contraception with few children. Since slum women do not show much diversification of their roles covering modern ones, opportunity cost does not seem to be relevant for them. Women falling under this category also are very rare. Hence, diversification of roles has no relevance in explaining the fertility behaviour of slum women. But it may be more relevant for non-slum women, which can be seen in a future study. In the light of distribution of these roles a negative association is noticed between roles of women and contraception.

migrant mothers, ... these roles [illegible] difficulties [illegible] assumptions and new roles, the opportunity [illegible] [illegible] [illegible] opportunity [illegible] fall under this category [illegible] of roles are sufficient to explain the fertility behaviour [illegible] women [illegible] more [illegible] than women [illegible] roles [illegible] between [illegible]

CHAPTER 7

PROGRAMME FACTORS AND CONTRACEPTIVE BEHAVIOUR

Government of India was the first in the world to adopt family planning as its official policy in 1951. The National Family Planning Programme started in 1951 with a clinical approach. Extension education approach was adopted in mid sixties and since late seventies, family planning delivery system has gradually expanded into a community oriented service approach. The programme has made a significant impact of fertility reduction. During 1970s, the birth rate declined from 40 to 34, but during 1979-84, it has been stagnating around 33. The programme is estimated to have averted about 70 million births in the country, upto the end of 1984-85. However, an overall couple protection rate of over 35 per cent has been achieved by 1985-86, and it was estimated at 37.5 per cent during 1987-88 (Family Welfare Year Book, 1988).

Various studies conducted through private and other organisations have highlighted that the existing infrastructure is not being optimally utilised mainly because of its inadequacies to provide proper services, and due to the relatively unfavourable attitude of the people towards it. The major inadequacies relate to poor quality of services, non-availability of staff, lack of sympathy of the staff and poor management (Ministry of Health and Family Welfare, 1985). Poor quality of services has resulted in relative under-utilization of facilities and lowering of the image and credibility of the health infrastructure. Improving facilities and upgrading the technical quality of services will, therefore, be a major need for widening the acceptance net of family planning. In this context, the present study has highlighted the following programme variables and their relationship with family planning adoption status. The variables considered here are : (1) place of last delivery; (2) persons who attended last delivery; (3) type of health centre visited;

(4) type of staff that gave service; (5) type of service rendered; (6) availability of services in an acceptable way; (7) proximity of the place of treatment and (8) opinion on incentives.

(1) *Place of Last Delivery :* This is one of the important factors which may influence the adoption of family planning. Generally, if the delivery takes place at the PHC (Primary Health Centre)/Hospital the tendency to use contraceptives will be more, because general types of PHC/Hospital staff, *viz.,* Doctors, Health visitors, ANM's (Auxiliary Nurse Midwife) and even trained 'dais' may motivate the concerned target couples directly or indirectly to use family planning methods. The present study also shows a positive relationship between hospital delivery and adoption of family planning (see Table 7.1). According to the present data it is interesting to note that 96.2 per cent of the respondents got their last child delivered at hospitals. On the other hand, only 3.8 per cent of them delivered their last child at their homes. This may be because the respondents of present study belong to the urban slum area and service facilities are easily available there. 50% of those whose last delivery was in a Govt. Hospital, adopted family planning, whereas the corresponding figure for those who had delivered their last child at home, was 47.8%.

Table 7.1 : **Place of Delivery of the Last Child**

Place of Delivery	*Adopters*	*Non-adopters*	*Total*	*%*
Home	47.8 (11)	52.2 (12)	100.0 (23)	3.8
Govt. Hospital	50.0 (289)	50.0 (288)	100.0 (577)	96.2
Total	50.0 (300)	50.0 (300)	100.0 (600)	100.0

Again when we consider the persons attending to deliveries in rural India, 80 per cent of the deliveries take place in the villages without help from any qualified persons, but attended to by locally available trained and untrained traditional birth attendants or midwives. They lack an understanding of health and ill-health. Therefore, their service is detrimental to maternal and child survival as well as adoption of family planning. Further, these local Dais may not intensively motivate the mothers to use family planning, since they themselves want deliveries to be conducted.

An analysis of the present data revealed that (Table 7.2) an overwhelming percentage (97%) of the births were attended to by either doctors or ANM's. Only a negligible percentage (3%) of the births were attended to by untrained persons. As mentioned above, this could be because of the respondents of the present study residing in urban slum areas. Again, when we consider the contraceptive behaviour of the respondents according to the type of birth attended, adoption status is slightly higher (50.5%) when their last deliveries were performed by doctors followed by ANMs (49.4%) and adoption status is only 44.4 per cent when their deliveries were performed by local dais. A reverse trend has been noticed for non-adopters.

Table 7.2 : Personnel attending to the Last Delivery

Person attending to the last delivery	*Adopters*	*Non-adopters*	*Total*	*%*
Dai	44.4 (8)	55.6 (10)	100.0 (18)	3.0
ANM	49.4 (83)	50.6 (85)	100.0 (168)	28.0
Doctor	50.5 (209)	49.5 (205)	100.0 (414)	69.0
Total	50.0 (300)	50.0 (300)	100.0 (600)	100.0

From these findings, it is confirmed that this difference was more striking in rural areas as compared to urban areas.

Type of Health Centres Visited : From Table 7.3 it is evident that a majority of the respondents (93.5%) had utilised the services of Government Hospitals during their last pregnancy followed by private hospitals (3.5%). On the other hand, only a negligible percentage (3%) of the respondents utilised the services of trained dais. However, a significant difference has been observed when we analyse the adoption status in relation to the type of health centre visited by the respondents. Among those who utilised the services of private hospitals, an overwhelming percentage (76.2%) of them adopted family planning, followed, by those who went to Government hospital (49.7%), but the least adoption status (27.8%) has been noticed among the respondents who have utilised the services of traditional Dais.

Table 7.3 : **Type of Health Centre Visited**

Type of health centre visited	*Adopters*	*Non-adopters*	*Total*	*%*
Traditional Dais	27.8 (5)	72.2 (13)	100.0 (18)	3.0
Private Hospital	76.2 (16)	23.8 (5)	100.0 (21)	3.5
Government Hospital	49.7 (299)	50.3 (282)	100.0 (561)	93.5
Total	50.0 (300)	50.0 (300)	100.0 (600)	100.0

X^2 = 9.334, sig. at .05 level.

Among the respondents who have utilised the services of traditional dais, 72.2 per cent were non-adopters of family planning as against 27.8 per cent who were adopters. However, of those who have utilised the services of private doctors, an overwhelming percentage (76.2%) had adopted contraception as against non-adopters (23.8%). At the same time, among the respondents who have utilised the services of Government hospitals an almost equal percentage of adopters and non-adopters have been observed.

From these findings, it can be concluded that the respondents seeking help from private hospitals were getting proper attention and motivation as compared to those who visited government hospitals.

Types of Services Rendered : An analysis of the type of services rendered by the health staff (Table 7.4), in general, revealed that the highest (52.3%) percentage of respondents had received the services of immunization and family planning advice, followed by 43.2 per cent who had received medical, immunization and family planning advice. However, only 4.5 per cent of the respondents received only a medical check-up, when we cross tabulate the variable with the family planning.

Adoption status of the respondents, as expected is the highest (54.4%) among those who received all the package of services, *viz.*, medical, immunization and family planning advice together, followed by 47 per cent among those received the services of immunization

Table 7.4 : **Type of Service Received**

Type of Service	*Adopters*	*Non-adopters*	*Total*	*%*
Medical Check-up only	40.7 (11)	59.3 (16)	100.0 (27)	4.5
Immunization and Family Planning Advice	47.1 (148)	52.9 (166)	100.0 (314)	52.3
Medical, immunization and family planning advice	54.4 (141)	45.6 (118)	100.0 (259)	43.2
Total	50.0 (300)	50.0 (300)	100.0 (600)	100.0

X^2 = 4.00; Not significant.

and family planning advice. Adoption status fell to the lowest percentage (40.7%) among those who received only medical check-up from the service personnel. A reverse trend has been observed among the non-adopters. From these findings, it can be confirmed that the use of contraception will be higher among those respondents, who received the health services coupled with the motivation of family planning.

Availability of Service in Acceptable Form : This is another important programme factor variable that influences contraception. The present study (Table 7.5) has shown a significant correlation between the availability of acceptable services and contraceptive adoption status.

In general 88.8 per cent of the respondents reported positively about the availability of service in acceptable form, while 11.2 per cent of them reported negatively. 51.6% of those who found that services were available in an acceptable form were adopters, whereas the corresponding percentage for those who found services unacceptable, was 37.3%. Thus the hypothesis that availability of acceptable services, leads to higher level of adoption of family planning, was confirmed here.

Table 7.5 : Availability of Service in Acceptable Form

Availability of service in acceptable form	*Adopters*	*Non-adopters*	*Total*	*%*
No	37.3 (25)	62.7 (42)	100.0 (67)	11.2
Yes	51.6 (275)	48.4 (258)	100.0 (533)	88.8
Total	50.0 (300)	50.0 (300)	100.0 (600)	100.0

X^2 = 4.856; Sig. at .05 level.

Proximity of Service Centre : For the effective utilization of the health and family planning, distance from the house of the respondent to the place of availability of service like sub-centre, PHC hospital etc., is a crucial factor. Of course, this distance again depends on the transportation system as well as on the effective motivation and services of the family planning workers. Generally, it is expected that the distance will have negative influence on the rate of adoption of family planning, i.e., lesser the distance higher the rate of adoption of family planning and vice versa. To test this hypothesis (here) data have been analysed accordingly and presented in Table 7.6.

Table 7.6 : Distance from the Residence to Family Planning Service Centres

Distance in Kms.	*Adopters*	*Non-adopters*	*Total*	*%*
≤ 1 Km.	34.5 (67)	65.5 (127)	100.0 (194)	32.3
1 - 2 Kms.	54.7 (151)	45.3 (125)	100.0 (276)	46.0
2 - 3 Kms.	55.9 (38)	44.1 (30)	100.0 (68)	11.3
4 Kms. +	71.0 (44)	29.0 (18)	100.0 (62)	10.3
Total	50.0 (300)	50.0 (300)	100.0 (600)	100.0

X^2 = 32.852, Sig. at. .01 level

From the last column of Table 7.6 it can be noticed that 46 per cent of the respondents are getting health and family welfare services within a distance of 1-2 Kms. from their residence. Another 32 per cent of them reported that the distance to the place of services (treatment) is less than one Km. However, some of them (11%) said that they are getting these services from about 2-3 Kms. range. Interestingly, only one-tenth of the respondents stated that they get the services from a distance of 3 or more Kms. Thus, it may be concluded that for a great majority (78.3%) of the respondents, the distance between their place of residence and the nearest centre is less than 2 Kms.

Proximity to Service Centre and Contraceptive Behaviour : Results from Table 7.6 surprisingly revealed that the percentage of family planning adopters increased from a lower level of 34.5 per cent to a higher level of 71% as the distance to the place of family planning service centre increased from less than one Km. to 3 Kms. or more. The expected hypothesis has been exactly reversed in the study area on account of the following reasons : (1) the transport system (especially the town buses) from Madras city of the slum areas is quite frequent and, therefore, a distance of 3 or 4 Kms., is not at all a major problem for getting satisfactory/sophisticated health and family planning services; (2) due to the arrangement of OTC programmes in the urban centres where Laproscope and well known lady doctors (Surgeons) were available at a distance of 4 to 5 Kms., (3) when OTC camps had been organised giving incentives and with involvement of voluntary agencies, transport to the OTC site was provided only to a selected few urban centres.

Satisfaction with Service Facilities (Index) : It is indeed a gigantic task in India to provide health and family planning services satisfactorily to all eligible couples. For measuring the respondents' satisfaction with service facilities they have been asked to reveal their opinions on different aspects of service facilities, and based on these opinions an index has been prepared (for details see the Chapter on Methodology). The respondents' level of satisfaction with service facilities (index) has been trichotomised into low, medium and high for the present investigation (see Table 7.7) and with these levels their contraceptive behaviour has been associated. For the present study, it is hypothesised that higher the level of respondents' satisfaction with the service facilities, higher will be the rate of adoption of family planning and vice versa.

In the study area, it is observed that around three-fifths (59%) of the respondents have had higher level of satisfaction with regard to the health and family planning service facilities available to them from various centres and family planning workers. It is a gratifying point for the service centres in the city. Another two-fifths (40%) of them also rated these facilities at moderate level. Interestingly, very negligible number (3%) of the respondents are of the opinion that these service facilities do not satisfy them. Thus, in the slum areas of Madras in general, the eligible couples have been provided by good health and family welfare services.

Table 7.7 : **Satisfaction with Service Facilities and Contraceptive Behaviour**

Index on service facilities	*Adopters*	*Non-adopters*	*Total*	*%*
Low level of satisfaction (6-8)	—	100.0 (3)	100.0 (3)	0.5
Medium level of satisfaction (9-11)	14.1 (34)	85.9 (207)	100.0 (241)	40.2
High level of satisfaction(12+)	74.7 (266)	25.3 (90)	100.0 (356)	59.3
Total	50.0 (300)	50.0 (300)	100.0 (600)	100.0

X^2 = 213.962; Sig. at .01 level.

Service Facilities (Index) and Contraceptive Behaviour

Looking at the differentials in contraceptive behaviour by the respondents' level of satisfaction with service facilities (index), it is fascinating to observe that the proportion of family planning adopters is very great (75%) among those respondents who responded with a very high level of satisfaction. On the other hand, the proportion is much less (14%) among those respondents who felt that the service facilities are moderately good. Interestingly, all the respondents (of course only 3) who are of the opinion that the service facilities are not satisfactory (low level) are non-adopters. These differentials in contraceptive behaviour by the respondents' level of satisfaction are also highly significant (x^2 = 213.962, Sig. at .01 level) and thus fully proved the hypothesis mentioned above in this regard. Based on these findings it may be suggested that health and family welfare services be made available to increase the rate of adoption of family planning tremendously as seen is this study.

Family Planning Adoption Status and Visits of Anganwadi

The credibility of peripheral level women's organisations like Anganwadi, Mahila Mandals and other voluntary agencies will have a positive influence on the adoption of family planning as well as maternal and child health. These organisations would interact with the eligible couples in their areas and provide them knowledge on health, immunization, family planning, nutrition services, etc. One of the recent studies conducted by Mahadevan and Sumangala (1987) also discovered the higher level of success rate among visitors to Anganwadi in family planning adoption. The present data also supports this hypothesis.

Table 7.8 : Family Planning Adoption Status by Visit to Anganwadi Centres

Anganwadi Visit	*Adopters*	*Non—adopters*	*Total*	*%*
No	41.1 (145)	58.9 (207)	100.0 (352)	58.7
Yes	62.5 (155)	37.5 (93)	100.0 (248)	41.3
Total	50.0 (300)	50.0 (300)	100.0 (600)	100.0

X^2 = 24.62; Sig. at .01 level.

In the total sample 41.3 per cent of the respondents used to visit Anganwadi as against 58.7 per cent who had not visited the centre. Further, as expected, of those who are visiting Anganwadi,

Table 7.9 : Family Planning Adopters' Status by Children attending Balwadi Centres

Children attending Balwadi	*Adopters*	*Non-adopters*	*Total*	*%*
No	44.3 (145)	55.7 (182)	100.0 (327)	54.5
Yes	56.8 (155)	43.2 (118)	100.0 (273)	45.5
Total	50.0 (300)	50.0 (300)	100.0 (600)	100.0

X^2 = 9.200, Sig, at .01 level.

62.5 per cent respondents adopted family planning, which is statistically significant (.01 level). Those who are not visiting Anganwadi show a reverse trend .

Again, when we analyse family planning adoption status according to respondent's children attending Balwadi, a direct relationship is noticed. In overall sample population 45.5 per cent of the respondents' children attend Balwadi (see Table 7.9). When we cross tabulate the same with their contraceptive adoption status, 56.8 per cent of them were adopters as against 44.3 per cent adopters whose children were not attending Balwadi. Here, again the difference is statistically significant (.01 level).

From this finding also we can suggest that Government should provide more grants for anganwadis and other voluntary agencies for strengthening their work. An integrated approach by the functionaries of various developmental departments at grass-root levels in promoting family planning will greatly enhance the promotion of family planning acceptance. Again, all these organisations, irrespective of their present field of operation, could be encouraged to work in the sphere of family welfare, and depending upon their capabilities, they can take up motivational and educational work as also the task of providing services.

Incentives and Family Planning

Incentives which directly motivate the clients and short circuit the normal human behaviour can influence fertility behaviour and play a crucial role in population control strategy. At present some incentives are available to the employees of central government, public sector undertakings and state governments in Madras city. Incentives will vary from state to state. Some states have introduced incentives in the form of lottery ticket and also as scheme of issuing green cards which entitle the acceptors of sterilization with two or less number of children to get special privileges for getting rations. In general, incentives play a positive role towards the adoption of family planning. For the present study, data have been collected from the respondents regarding their opinions on female incentives, *viz.,* incentives given to tubectomy and loop. Respondents' knowledge of other incentives and whether they have received the incentives or not and their effect on the adoption of family planning have been presented here.

According to Table 7.10 the respondents' opinion on female incentives, *viz.,* tubectomy and loop in relation to their adoption status has been ascertained.

In general 69.8 per cent of respondents gave the opinion that the female incentives were sufficient as against only 14.3 per cent who felt that they were inadequate. Of course, 20.8 per cent of them were not aware of incentives. While describing the incentives for Tubectomy in relation to family planning adoption status a

Table 7.10 : Opinions on Incentives to Females

Types of incentives	*Adopters*	*Non-adopters*	*Total*	*%*
I. Incentives for Tubectomy				
D.K./N.A.	8.0 (10)	92.0 (115)	100.0 (125)	20.8
Less	94.2 (81)	5.8 (5)	100.0 (86)	14.3
Sufficient	53.7 (209)	46.3 (180)	100.0 (389)	69.8
		X^2 = 48.470; Sig. at .01 level		
II. Incentives for Loop				
D.K./N.A.	13.8 (21)	86.2 (131)	100.0 (152)	25.3
Less	53.4 (47)	46.6 (41)	100.0 (88)	14.7
Sufficient	64.4 (232)	35.6 (128)	100.0 (360)	60.0
Total	50.0 (300)	50.0 (300)	100.0 (600)	100.0

X^2 = 3.860 ; Sig. at .01 level.

D.K. = Don't know
N.A. = Not available

significant difference has been noticed. Among the respondents who are not aware of the incentives, as expected, the adoption status was very low (8%)). Of the respondents who rated the incentives as inadequate, as many as 94.2% were nevertheless adopters. On the other hand 53.7 per cent of those with the opinion that the incentives were sufficient were adopters.

64.4% of those who found incentives for loop to be sufficient were adopters, as against 53.4% adopters amongst those who found the incentives to be inadequate. The adoption status is significantly less (13.8%) for those who have no knowledge about the incentives.

Table 7.11 : **Knowledge Regarding other Incentives and Adoption Status**

Knowledge regarding other incentives	*Adopters*	*Non-adopters*	*Total*	*%*
Not known	31.8 (28)	68.2 (60)	100.0 (88)	14.7
Known	53.1 (272)	46.9 (240)	100.0 (512)	85.3
Total	50.0 (300)	50.0 (300)	100.0 (600)	100.0

X^2 = 13.636; Sig. at .01 level.

Data presented in Table 7.11 depicts the knowledge regarding incentives other than those offered for tubectomy and loop. On the whole, 85.3 per cent of the respondents expressed the knowledge about other incentives as against only 14.7 per cent who are not aware of it. The same pattern is seen when we analyse their adoption status (.01% level).

Table 7.12 : **Did you Receive any Incentives**

Received any incentives or not	*Adopters*	*Non-adopters*	*Total*	*%*
N.A.	1.6 (4)	98.4 (243)	100.0 (247)	50.6
No	40.0 (38)	60.0 (57)	100.0 (95)	6.3
Yes	100.0 (258)	—	100.0 (258)	43.1
Total	50.0 (300)	50.0 (300)	100.0 (600)	100.0

Table 7.12 shows the incentives received by the respondents across their adoption status. Here, it is interesting to note that of those who have not received incentives, 40 per cent adopted family planning. This may be because of the impact of education and

motivation other than through incentives. Also, during the interview with them, it was known that their programme for adoption was in the private hospitals. Hence, it is certain that they adopted contraception exclusively on the basis of the need for limiting family size. The services for health problems availed by these respondents were from the private hospitals only. As expected, cent per cent of those who received incentives adopted contraception. All these support the argument that incentives may have to be given to the illiterate population like slum dwellers to expedite the acceptance of contraception. In fact, the rate of incentive may also be enhanced to strengthen the family planning programme along with effective and continuous education and motivation.

[illegible]

CHAPTER 8

COMMUNICATION AND CONTRACEPTIVE BEHAVIOUR

Interpersonal Communication

Generally, people receive information on family planning from several interpersonal channels as well as from sources of mass media. It has been confirmed by several empirical studies that interpersonal sources are relatively more effective in disseminating family planning information than the mass media (Rogers, 1962; Mahadevan, 1984; Thangadurai, 1987). Interpersonal sources not only impart awareness to the clients, but also motivate them extensively to accept contraception. On the other hand, mass media largely develops awareness and is not as effective in influencing the adoption of contraception. Therefore, in the present study an attempt has been made to find out the various interpersonal sources of family planning communication and also their influence on adoption process (see Table 8.1).

Of all the inter-personal sources of communication, family planning workers have played the major role in communication (81%) in imparting family planning information to the respondents, followed by the satisfied adopters (52%). Fewer respondents reported that they received family planning information from their relatives (29%) as well as from the voluntary workers (15%) and from their neighbours/friends (12%). Only 9 per cent and 7 per cent of the respondents respectively mentioned that they got the information from dissatisfied adopters and other workers, *viz.,* health visitor, supervisors, etc. The former source is a dangerous one for the interest of promoting the programme and may have to be viewed seriously to prevent such cases in future.

Looking at the differentials in the adoption status by the respondents' sources of family planning information (see Table 8.1) it is evident that the percentage of adopters is comparatively higher

Table 8.1 : Interpersonal Sources of Communication and Contraceptive Behaviour

Source of family planning information	*Adopters*	*Non-adopters*	*Total*	%
1. *Neighbours/Friends*				
Not received	49.0 (259)	51.0 (270)	100.0 (529)	88.2
Received	57.7 (41)	42.3 (30)	100.0 (71)	11.8
2. *Relatives*				
Not Received	51.9 (222)	48.1 (206)	100.0 (428)	71.3
Received	45.3 (78)	54.7 (94)	100.0 (172)	28.7
3. *Adopters (Satisfied)*				
Not received	46.4 (135)	53.6 (156)	100.0 (291)	48.5
Received	53.4 (165)	46.6 (144)	100.0 (309)	51.5
4. *Dissatisfied Adopters*				
Not received	49.4 (270)	50.6 (277)	100.0 (547)	91.2
Received	56.6 (30)	43.4 (23)	100.0 (53)	8.8
5. *Family Planning*				
Not received	47.5 (42)	52.5 (70)	100.0 (112)	18.7
Received	52.9 (258)	47.1 (230)	100.0 (488)	81.3
6. *Voluntary Workers*				
Not received	49.6 (252)	50.4 (256)	100.0 (508)	84.7
Received	52.2 (48)	47.8 (44)	100.0 (92)	15.3
7. *Other Workers (Specify)*				
Not received	49.5 (277)	50.5 (283)	100.0 (560)	93.3
Received	57.5 (23)	42.5 (17)	100.0 (40)	6.7
Total	50.0 (300)	50.0 (300)	100.0 (600)	100.0

when they received family planning information from one or more interpersonal sources, rather than if they did not receive any information from these sources. However, an opposite trend in this regard is noticed when they got information from the relatives. Another surprising feature noticed is that the percentage of adopters is comparatively higher among those respondents who received family planning information from the dissatisfied adopters too. However, these differentials in adoption status by source of communication in family planning are not statistically significant.

Nevertheless, two types of generalisations emerge out of the present empirical findings as given in Table 8.1. Relatively more adopters emerge than non-adopters, when they receive information on family planning from several sources. It supports the policy option that multi-media channels and preferably interpersonal sources form a feasible and favourable factor to be encouraged in this programme. While the extent of coverage and influence of most of the interpersonal sources helped adopters for contraception, dissatisfied early adopters and relatives did not promote family planning on similar lines. In fact more of them communicated with the non-adopters than adopters.

Importance of Inter-personal Sources

After ascertaining the sources of inter-personal communication on family planning, the respondents were asked to state name of the source, which they believe to be the most important one. This information is essential because these important sources may have influence on their immediate adoption/non-adoption of family planning which can be seen in Table 8.2.

For understanding the differential importance of the determinants of adoption status, particularly of the sources of family planning communication, the respondents were asked to state the name of the source, which they believe to be the most important one. This information is essential because of their expected diverse influence on their immediate adoption/non-adoption of family planning, which can be seen in Table 8.2. On the whole, an overwhelming proportion of the respondents (87.5%) stated that they gave more importance to the message provided to them by the satisfied adopters. Their percentage is also more among adopters (52.2%) than non-adopters (47.8%). Very negligible (6.5%) other sources were found to be important to respondents. Preference given to neighbours and relatives was also very negligible (4.8%). For the present study, it has been hypothesised that the rate of family planning would be higher for those respondents, who believe that information received from satisfied adopters is more important than neighbours and relatives and all other sources of communication, which is proved here. Therefore, it may be suggested that satisfied adopters, have to be encouraged to disseminate more credible information to the target couples to strengthen family planning programme.

Table 8.2 : Most Important Interpersonal Sources of Communication and Contraception Behaviour

Sources	*Adopters*	*Non-adopters*	*Total*	*%*
Not applicable	14.3 (1)	85.7 (6)	100.0 (7)	1.2
Adopters	52.2 (274)	47.8 (251)	100.0 (525)	87.5
Neighbours and Relatives	58.6 (17)	41.4 (12)	100.0 (29)	4.8
Others@	20.5 (8)	79.5 (31)	100.0 (39)	6.5

X^2 = 15.4566; Sig. at. .01 level.
@ Dissatisfied adopters, family planning and other voluntary workers.

Mass Media Sources and Contraceptive Behaviour

The respondents were asked about the most familiar type of mass media sources of family planning information. The responses are given in Table 8.3. Of all the sources of mass media, radio has been mentioned extensively by the respondents (58.5%) followed by films (30%). Only a negligible 6.5 per cent of the respondents stated various other mass media sources, *viz.,* newspapers, wall-posters, etc. Unexpectedly around 5 per cent of the respondents claimed that they do not like any mass media channels of family planning communication.

In order to find out the type of familiar mass media channels which may have certain influence on the adoption of family planning, data have been analysed and presented in Table 8.3. It is interesting to note that the percentage of adopters is significantly (X^2 = 21.0386;

Table 8.3 : Types of Mass Media Sources of Communication and Contraceptive Behaviour

Mass Media	*Adopters*	*Non-adopters*	*Total*	*%*
Not liking any mass media	20.0 (6)	80.0 (24)	100.0 (30)	5.0
Radio	56.7 (199)	43.3 (152)	100.0 (351)	58.5
Films	43.9 (79)	56.1 (101)	100.0 (180)	30.0
Others (Newspapers, Wall-posters etc.)	41.0 (16)	59.0 (23)	100.0 (39)	6.5
Total	50.0 (300)	50.0 (300)	100.0 (600)	100.0

X^2 = 21.0386; Sig. at 1 per cent level.

Sig. at .01 level) high (57%) among those respondents who received message from radio as the source of family planning information than those respondents who received the message through films (44%) and 'other' mass media sources (41%). Thus, among the respondents belonging to Madras slum areas radio plays an important role in disseminating message of family planning. Though the outreach of message on family planning is greater through radio, which is expected, it cannot alone be sufficient to motivate couples for contraception. This is evident when this table is compared with Table 8.1. Further intensive study exclusively on mass media and interpersonal sources of communication is needed to confirm the relative importance of these channels of communication.

Satisfaction with Media Availability

After enquiring about the most familiar mass media sources, the respondents of the present study were further asked to state whether they are satisfied with the availability of various mass media channels for disseminating message on family planning. Information with regard to this aspect is provided in Table 8.4. On the whole, an overwhelming percentage (84%) of the respondents are quite satisfied with the availability of various mass media sources that are imparting family planning information. The rest of them (16%) did not agree on the satisfactory availability of mass media for this purpose.

In order to know whether their level of satisfaction with regard to the mass media will have any influence on their family planning adoption status data have been analysed and presented in Table 8.4. It is clear from this table that the percentage of adopters is

Table 8.4 : **Satisfaction with Respect to Mass Media Availability and Contraceptive Behaviour**

Satisfaction with Media Availability	*Adopters*	*Non-adopters*	*Total*	*%*
Not satisfied	43.9 (43)	56.1 (55)	100.0 (98)	16.3
Satisfied	51.2 (257)	48.8 (245)	100.0 (502)	83.7
Total	50.0 (300)	50.0 (300)	100.0 (600)	100.0

X^2 = 1.7562; N.S.

comparatively higher (51%) among those respondents who are satisfied with the overall availability of the various mass media sources in the study area, than among those respondents who are not satisfied (44%) with it. However, these differentials in the adoption status are not statistically significant.

Willingness to Motivate other Clients

After obtaining family planning information through one or the other sources of media it is quite natural that people may share, discuss and even motivate the other couples like neighbours, relatives and friends to adopt one or the other methods of family planning. Therefore, the respondents have been asked to state whether they will motivate any of their relatives, neighbours and friends after receiving family planning information from different media (Table 8.5). Since a good proportion of couples who adopted contraception is willing to motivate others, earnest efforts may be made to involve them in the ongoing family planning programme. Since satisfied adopters are the best credible sources of communication, urgent efforts are needed in this direction.

A glance at Table 8.5, reveals that an overwhelming proportion of the respondents (91%) have agreed that they will motivate their neighbours, relatives and friends after receiving family planning information through various mass media channels. Results from Table 8.5 reveal that the percentage of the adopters, is significantly (X^2 = 11.721; Sig. at. .01 level) greater (52%) among those respondents who are interested in motivating their neighbours, relatives and friends towards family planning as compared to those respondents who are not interested in motivating these members (28%). As expected most of the non-adopters are not willing to motivate other couples for contraception.

Table 8.5 : Motivating Others after Obtaining Family Planning Information Through Media, and Contraceptive Behaviour

Motiving others after obtaining information regarding family planning	*Adopters*	*Non-adopters*	*Total*	*%*
Will not motivate	27.8 (15)	72.2 (39)	100.0 (54)	9.0
Will motivate	52.2 (285)	47.8 (261)	100.0 (546)	91.0
Total	50.0 (300)	50.0 (300)	100.0 (600)	100.0

X^2 = 11.721; Sig. at .01 level.

Attending Orientation Camps

As part of their job, the family planning staff conduct orientation camps for the target couples with regard to various methods of family planning to educate them on these methods. Those couples, who attend this programme, may adopt family planning, since they would be intensively educated with the basic knowledge about all the methods. Therefore, we hypothesize that the rate of adoption will be higher among those couples, who attended these orientation camps than among those who did not attend the same. To examine this hypothesis, the respondents have been asked to state whether they, or their spouses have attended any orientation camp (Table 8.6).

Looking at the data provided in Table 8.6, it is clear that slightly more than one-third (35%) of the respondents (or their spouses) attended the orientation camps, as against 65 per cent who did not attend any such camps. It speaks about the poor coverage of OTC camps. As expected, the rate of family planning adoption is

Table 8.6 : Attendance at Orientation Camps (OTCS) and Contraceptive Behaviour

Attended OTC or not	*Adopters*	*Non-adopters*	*Total*	*%*
Not attended	45.6 (178)	54.4 (212)	100.0 (390)	65.0
Attended	58.1 (122)	41.9 (88)	100.0 (210)	35.0
Total	50.0 (300)	50.0 (300)	100.0 (600)	100.0

X^2 = 8.4690; Sig. at .01 level.

significantly (at 0.01 level) higher (58%) among those respondents, who attended one or the other orientation camp. Similarly a significant proportion did not adopt contraception, when the respondents did not get exposure to OTC camps. Hence, it is plausible that participation in OTC camps enables many people to accept contraception. However, a review of OTC camps and their effectiveness is needed since 41.9 per cent of the clients did not accept despite attending OTC camps.

Awareness of Success Cases in Contraceptive Behaviour

In the process of family planning communication and motivation, the instances of successful adoption of contraception, that too by credible and familiar cases, will have a greater positive influence on the target couples, who too may adopt it soon. Therefore, in the present study the respondents were asked to state whether or not they heard stories of successful adoption of family planning by people in their area and this information was cross tabulated with their family planning adoption status (Table 8.7). In the study area, around 39 per cent of the respondents replied that they heard the stories of success, whereas the rest 61 per cent mentioned that they did not hear of cases of successful family planning adoption in their area (Table 8.7).

Looking at the influence of knowledge of stories of successful adoption of family planning, it is clear that the percentage of adopters is decisively higher (64%) among those respondents who had heard stories of success, than among those respondents who did not hear these (41%). An exact reverse trend is noticed in the case of non-adopters of family planning. Further, it is fascinating to observe that these differentials in the adoption status by knowledge of stories of success are statistically significant (X^2 = 30.5246; Sig. at .01 level). Based on these results it may be inferred that the information about the stories of successful family planning adoption cases may be disseminated through various channels of communication and may be cited by all the family planning workers etc. in motivating the target couples towards adoption of family planning.

Table 8.7 : Influence of Knowledge of Stories of Successful Adoption of Contraception

Heard of successful stories	*Adopters*	*Non-adopters*	*Total*	*%*
Not heard	41.0 (149)	59.0 (215)	10.0 (364)	60.7
Heard	63.9 (151)	36.1 (85)	100.0 (236)	39.3
Total	50.0 (300)	50.0 (300)	100.0 (600)	100.0

X^2 = 30.5246; Sig. at .01 level.

Fear of Adoption and Contraceptive Behaviour

Though the dissemination of stories of success will lead to higher rate of family planning adoption, fear of adoption of family planning may play a critical role as an obstacle. This may be because the dissemination of adverse effect or failure or problems of contraception. Psychologically, people will respond immediately to the bad effect rather than to a good influence. Once they hear stories of failure or of side effects of family planning adoption, target couples will perceive that the adoption of family planning is bad and thus may develop a psychological aversion towards the adoption of family planning which may lead to non-adoption of family planning. Keeping this point in view the respondents have been asked if they had any fear of adoption of family planning due to any information they had about any adverse aspect of family planning. Their responses are given in Table 8.8. Interestingly, only one-sixth of the respondents replied that they are afraid of adoption of family planning whereas the remaining greater proportion (84%) of them stated that they do not have any fear towards the adoption of family planning.

A glance at Table 8.8 further reveals that the percentage of adopters is significantly (X^2 = 9.8898; Sig. at .01 level) lower (35%)

among those respondents who have the fear of adoption as compared to those respondents who are not afraid of family planning adoption (53%). Based on these results it may be concluded that fear of adoption will have a negative influence on adoption of family planning. Under these circumstances it may be suggested that utmost care has to be taken by the family planning workers to eliminate this fear of adoption from the target couples at the earliest.

Table 8.8 : Fear of Adoption and Contraceptive Behaviour

Fear of adoption	*Adopters*	*Non-adopters*	*Total*	*%*
No	52.8 (267)	47.3 (239)	100.0 (506)	84.3
Yes	35.1 (33)	64.9 (61)	100.0 (94)	15.7
Total	50.0 (300)	50.0 (300)	100.0 (600)	100.0

X^2 = 9.8898; Sig. at .01 level.

Discussion with Satisfied Adopters

Satisfied adopters of family planning play a vital role for the effective implementation of family planning programme. Discussion with these satisfied adopters by the eligible couples may create favourable attitude among them, which in turn may lead to the adoption of family planning. Hence, we may expect higher rate of

Table 8.9 : Discussion with Satisfied Adopters and Contraceptive Behaviour

Discussion with satisfied field adopters	*Adopters*	*Non-adopters*	*Total*	*%*
Not discussed	33.1 (86)	66.9 (174)	100.0 (260)	43.3
Discussed	62.9 (214)	37.1 (126)	100.0 (340)	56.7
Total	50.0 (300)	50.0 (300)	100.0 (600)	100.0

X^2 = 52.5610; Sig. at .01 level.

adoption among those group of respondents who discuss with the satisfied adopters as against those who do not. Information with regard to this is provided in Table 8.9. Among the total sample majority of the respondents (57%) said that they have had discussion with satisfied adopters and the rest of them (43%) answered that they did not.

Data from Table 8.9, confirmed the hypothesis that the percentage of adopters is significantly greater (63%) among the group of respondents, who discussed with the satisfied adopters than among those respondents who did not discuss with satisfied adopters (33%). These differentials are statistically significant (X^2 = 52.5610; Sig. at .01 level) and thus fully support the expected hypothesis.

Discussion with Family Planning Workers and Contraceptive Behaviour

For the successful practice of family planning, discussion regarding family planning matters between the concerned spouses is essential. Some of the studies have conclusively proved that the rate of adoption of family planning will be higher among those couples who discuss family planning than among those who do not (Stycos, et al., 1954; Poffenberger, 1969; Pillai, 1971; U.N. 1975; Khan, 1979; Sivaraju, 1987). To test this hypothesis in this study area, data has been analysed accordingly and given in Table 8.10.

Table 8.10 : **Family Planning Discussion among the Couple**

Family planning discussion among the couple	*Adopters*	*Non-adopters*	*Total*	*%*
Not discussed	53.7 (254)	46.3 (219)	100.0 (473)	78.8
Discussed	36.2 (46)	63.8 (81)	100.0 (127)	21.2
Total	50.0 (300)	50.0 (300)	100.0 (600)	100.0

X^2 = 12.2354; Sig. at .01 level.

From Table 8.10 it is clear that only 21 per cent of the respondents have discussed family planning with their husbands whereas the rest of them did not do so (79%). Thus, in the study (slum) area of Madras city, communication between the couple about family planning is very poor. The reason is that the adopters, specially women, did not share spouse communication but accepted family planning due to the high motivation during the camps.

With regard to the relationship between family planning discussion among couples and contraceptive behaviour, data has been presented in Table 8.10; surprisingly the hypothesis is not confirmed. For instance, the percentage of adopters is significantly (X^2 = 12.2354; Sig. at .01 level) higher (54%) among those couples who reported that they never discussed family planning than among those who discussed it (35%). This is because the slum women have greater autonomy in decision making since they earn like their husbands. Hence, the respondents have acted on their own accord illustrating the effectiveness of individual decision making, which is not there in other rural areas.

Frequency of Motivation and Contraceptive Behaviour

Contraceptive behaviour may also be influenced by the frequency of contact and motivation either through family planning workers or through doctors. As a general practice family planning workers motivate the eligible couples to adopt one or the other methods of family planning for their family welfare. Human behaviour is such that an innovation will not be adopted at the first instance and repeated motivation towards that innovation is essential to successfully make it acceptable. Therefore, we may expect that as the frequency of motivation increases, the rate of adoption of family planning also increases. To test this hypothesis in the present study, data has been analysed and presented in Table 8.11.

An analysis of contraceptive behaviour of the respondents by the frequency of motivation (Table 8.11) by family planning workers suggests that the percentage of adopters is comparatively higher (60%) among those couples who have been motivated just once, whereas the percentage is somewhat less for couples who have been motivated more than once (45%) and on several occasions (51%). The X^2 results also showed that the differentials in contraceptive behaviour by the frequency of motivation, are moderately significant. Of course, largest number of respondents adopted contraception when they were contacted more than once by the workers. Therefore, repeated efforts of motivation by workers are needed to motivate illiterate population like slum dwellers to accept contraception.

Table 8.11 : Frequency of Motivation by Family Planning Workers on Family Planning and Family Planning Adoption Status

Frequency of motivation	*Adopters*	*Non-adopters*	*Total*	*%*
Once	60.0 (60)	40.0 (40)	100.0 (100)	16.7
More than once	44.9 (111)	55.1 (136)	100.0 (247)	41.2
Several times	51.0 (129)	49.0 (124)	100.0 (253)	42.1
Total	50.0 (300)	50.0 (300)	100.0 (600)	100.0

X^2 = 6.6292; Sig. at .05 level.

CHAPTER 9

DEMOGRAPHIC CHARACTERISTICS AND FAMILY PLANNING STATUS

Demographic variables constitute a major category of factors that influenced the contraceptive behaviour as seen in a number of earlier studies (Siddique, 1965; Srinivasan & Kachirayan, 1968; Presser and Bumpass, 1970). The present chapter deals with demographic characteristics and their influences on the sample respondents and their family planning adoption status. The demographic characteristics considered here are : age at marriage of the respondents, duration of marriage, number of living children and duration of breastfeeding in relation to contraceptive behaviour.

Age at Marriage of Wife (Respondents)

Age at marriage of females is one of the important demographic variables influencing the family planning adoption status. Now, it has been widely acclaimed that early age at marriage of women invariably is one of the major demographic factors that accounts for more pregnancies, more maternal deaths and low adoption rate of family planning. A few studies have documented that late age at marriage of women effectively increases their awareness and interest in family planning besides creating favourable attitude towards different family planning methods. These changes in turn will lead to adoption of one or the other method of family planning (Morrison, 1956; Fatima, 1977 ; Bhatia, 1979, 1983, 1984 ; Audinarayana 1981, 1986; Sivaraju, 1982; Arora, 1983; Bhuyan and Bhuyan, 1984). Therefore, for the present study, it has been hypothesised that age at marriage of the respondents will have a positive influence on the adoption of family planning. To examine this hypothesis data have been analysed accordingly and presented in Table 9.1.

The proportion of women married at 18 or later years, which is the legally eligible age at marriage of girls, constitutes the majority of women (55%) in this population. Further age-wise break-up revaeals that age at marriage is not generally low among most of the women except for the very low age at marriage noticed among 16.5 per cent women who married at 15 years or less.

Table 9.1 : Percentage Distribution of Family Planning and Age at Marriage of Wife

Age at marriage	*Adoption*	*Non-adoption*	*Total*	*%*
≤-15 years	54.5 (54)	45.5 (45)	100.0 (99)	16.5
16-17 years	57.3 (98)	42.7 (73)	100.0 (171)	28.5
18-19 years	46.0 (98)	54.0 (115)	100.0 (213)	35.5
20+ years	42.7 (50)	57.3 (67)	100.0 (117)	19.5
Total	50.0 (300)	50.0 (300)	100.0 (600)	100.0

From the preceding Table 9.1, it is evident that slightly more than one-third of the respondents (35.5%) in the study area, got married at the ages of 18-19 years and another one-fifth of them (19.5%) married at somewhat late ages (20+ years). The pity is that over a quarter of them got married at the early ages of 16-17 years (28.5%) besides 16.5 per cent who got married at 15 years or less. Thus around 45 per cent of them married earlier than the legally prescribed age of 18 years. Of course most of these people married long before the recent legislation regarding age at marriage came into being in 1978. Hence, it is not right to compare the appropriateness of age at marriage of these women in the light of a legislation enacted later on.

With regard to the relationship between age at marriage and family planning adoption status, surprisingly there exists an exact negative association between these two variables under consideration. For instance, the percentage of adopters is relatively higher (55% and 57% respectively) among the respondents, who got married at comparatively early ages (15 years and 16-17 years respectively), which has decreased to 46 and then to 43, when their age at marriage increased to 18-19 years and 20 and more years respectively. More young women who married early would have adopted contraception because of the difficulty they now face out of high fertility. Therefore, the influence is not exclusively of age at marriage per se, but of high fertility incentive etc. But among the non-adopters, age at marriage shows an inconsistent trend.

Duration of Marriage : Duration of married life will also influence the adoption of family planning status. Generally, members with long duration of married life are likely to adopt one or the other method of family planning than the members with short duration of married life. This may be because the former group may already have more number of children and may also have achieved their desired family size with desired sex-combination of the children.

Very few studies have supported this positive association between duration of married life and family planning adoption. However, some of the studies conducted in India and abroad have exhibited a significant positive association between the number of living children and the acceptance of contraception. These studies (Hoffman and Wyatt, 1960), Rainwater, 1960; U.N. 1961; Caldwell, 1967; Arnold, 1975; Khan, 1979) observed the importance of another important determinant of contraception, i.e., value of dimensions for desiring more number of children during the long period of reproduction. Caldwell (1968) observed that children are economically valuable and share the burden of work and they provide the much needed assistance in families. However, a few studies have shown that there is a positive association between the age at marriage, duration of married life of women and the effective increase in their awareness, interest and creates an unfavourable attitude towards different family planning methods which in turn will lead to adopt one or the other methods of family planning (Morrison, 1956; Audinarayana, 1981, 1986; Sivaraju, 1982). To examine whether such association is existing in the present study, data has been analysed accordingly and given in Table 9.2.

On the whole, slightly more than half of the respondents (53%) have experienced a duration of married life of 10 years or less, whereas 41 per cent of them have experienced duration of married life of 11-20 years, and only 6 per cent of them have experienced a married life of 21 or more respectively.

As expected, data from Table 9.2 suggest that there exists a positive association between the duration of married life and adoption of family planning. For the youngest category of duration

Table 9.2 : Duration of Married Life and Family Planning Adoption Status

Duration of married life	*Adoption*	*Non-adoption*	*Total*	*%*
10 years	42.3 (135)	57.7 (184)	100.0 (319)	53.2
11-20 years	56.5 (140)	43.5 (108)	100.0 (248)	41.3
21+ years	75.8 (25)	24.2 (8)	100.0 (33)	5.5
Total	50.0 (300)	50.0 (300)	100.0 (600)	100.0

X^2 = 20.414; Sig. at .01 level.

of married life of women with 10 years, only 42 per cent adopted contraception. Percentage of adopters has increased to 57 per cent and then to 76 per cent when the duration of their married life increased to 11-20 years and then to 21 or more years. An exact reverse trend is noticed in the case of non-adopters. The difference in adoption/non-adoption of family planning methods by duration of married life are also statistically highly significant (X^2 = 20.414; Sign. at .01 level) and thus confirmed the aforesaid hypothesis. These findings are also analogous with some of the findings of the earlier studies.

Number of living children : It is generally believed that eligible couples may adopt one or the other methods of family planning mostly after getting at least two or more living children. Therefore, we can expect that the number of living children may exhibit a positive influence on the adoption of family planning. To test this hypothesis in the present study, data on family planning status has been cross-tabulated with the number of living children and presented in Table 9.3.

Half of the respondents (49.5%) in the study area, have three or more number of living children, and another 47 per cent of them have two living children but only 4 per cent of them have single child. This clearly shows that still half of the people in the slum areas of Madras city are having three or more children at the time of their adoption of contraception. This is because the overwhelming numbers of the respondents are found to be either illiterate or having attained only primary level of education.

Table 9.3 : Number of Living Children and Family Planning Adoption Status

Number of living children	*Adopters*	*Non-Adopters*	*Total*	*%*
One	36.4 (8)	63.6 (14)	100.0 (22)	3.7
Two	37.0 (104)	63.0 (177)	100.0 (281)	46.8
Three +	63.3 (188)	36.7 (109)	100.0 (297)	49.5
Total	50.0 (300)	50.0 (300)	100.0 (600)	100.0

The hypothesis that there exists a positive relationship between the number of living children and adoption of contraception has been confirmed here as per the findings in Table 9.3. For example, the percentage of adopters is only 36 and 37 per cent respectively among the respondents, who have one and two children, but this proportion has almost doubled among those respondents who have three or more living children. On the other hand, the corresponding percentages of non-adopters showed a negative relationship with number of living children. While the proportion of non-adopters constitute only 37 per cent for couples with three and more living children, it accounted for 64 per cent couples with one living child. Similar findings are also observed in some of the other studies conducted in different parts of India (Khan, 1979; Reddy, 1984 and Reddy, 1985).

Sex Combination of Living Children

In addition to the total number of living children, the sex combination of children also will have a great influence on the adoption of contraceptive methods. In general, the eligible couples may try to adopt one or the other family planning methods after getting the desired combination of 1 male + 1 female or 2 male + 1 or 2 female children. Further, couples generally practice family planning when they have more number of male children as against female children and thus give greater value for sons rather than daughters. In addition, the rate of use of family planning methods in general, will be less among those couples who have higher number of female children as compared to male children. These are the expected hypothesis which we have examined here in the context of male preference in the male dominated society like India. To observe whether these determinants are found true in the present study, data have been analysed accordingly and presented in Table 9.4.

Table 9.4 : Sex Combination of the Living Children and Contraceptive Acceptance

Sex combination of living children	*Adopters*	*Non-adopters*	*Total*	*%*
No male + one female	10.0 (1)	90.0 (9)	100.0 (10)	1.7
One male + no female	26.9 (7)	73.1 (19)	100.0 (26)	4.3
No male + two female	34.5 (19)	65.5 (36)	100.0 (55)	9.2
Two male + no female	38.6 (22)	61.4 (35)	100.0 (57)	9.5
One male + one female	40.9 (63)	59.1 (91)	100.0 (154)	25.7
Total three + with males less than females	59.5 (72)	40.5 (49)	100.0 (121)	20.2
3+ with equal or more males than females	65.5 (116)	34.5 (61)	100.0 (177)	29.5
Total	(300)	(300)	(600)	(100)

Influence of value of children on contraceptive use has shown a consistent direct relationship and an opposite relationship in case of non-adopters. The rate of adoption has gone up to as high as 65.5 per cent when the couples got 3 or more living children including sons. For such population, the per cent of non adopters happens to be lowest, i.e., 34.5. When the adopters and non-adopters are compared among couples with no male child, very significant difference is noticed. Similar situation existed for couples with one male and no female or with no male and only female children. When the couples got 2 male + no female children, non-adopters (61%)

outnumber adopters (39%). Many couples also could not be satisfied with one male and one female child because in such categories, when 59 per cent of them did not adopt contraception, only 41 per cent adopted it. However, amongst couples with 3+ children, having more daughters than sons, a greater proportion (59.5%) is seen to adopt family planning rather than avoid it (40%). It is because of the concern and difficulty involved in arranging their marriage in future because of the burden of dowry. It is not due to positive value in this regard. Thus the hypothesis said above was more or less confirmed in the study. In other words there is a definite sex preference among couples influencing/not influencing them to adopt one or the other method of contraceptive. These preferences are weighed in favour of greater number of sons and not daughters. The critical level of son preference is around 2 to 3 sons. But the number of daughters in the family is not a major determinant of contraception.

CHAPTER 10

SUMMARY AND REGRESSION FINDINGS

This empirical study is the outcome of a retrospective survey conducted among slum dwellers of Madras city during 1987. The study has been carried out to examine the importance of various factors : cultural, socio-economic, demographic, modernization, status of women, communication and family planning programme variables that influence behaviour with regard to contraception of slum dwellers (women) of Madras city. Further, it rightly covered both the adopters and non-adopters of contraception to examine the major determinants of their behaviour. Studies conducted on determinants of contraceptive behaviour effects among the slum dwellers are very meagre in India and nil in Madras city. Therefore, this study is innovative and comprehensive in its coverage of conventional and new variables. The regression findings given here further strengthen the generalisations made in this summary chapter.

Methodology : A total sample of 600 slum dwellers who form the respondents (women) - 300 adopters and 300 non-adopters have been selected at random from Madras city. A multistage random sample technique was followed for the selection of respondents. At the first stage of selection, out of the 150 wards of Madras city, 99 wards were purposively selected on the basis on the following criteria *viz.*, (i) wards with family planning centres and (ii) wards with women's voluntary service centres. In the second stage, out of the these 99 selected wards, elgible couples were listed out separately as adopters and non-adopters. Out of them, 300 adopters and 300 non-adopter couples were selected at random. However, for the present study women alone were considered as respondents. Data were collected from the respondents using a detailed interview schedule exclusively prepared for this purpose. The collected data were analysed using computer facility. Frequency tables and cross tabulations were made for presenting the data. The X^2 test was used to test the association between the independent and dependent variables. The dependent variable is the contraceptive behaviour for both the adopters and non-adopters of family planning. In addition to this, a step-wise regression analysis was carried out to know the regression co-efficients to ascertain the nature of causal relationship of various factors on the contraceptive behaviour, and the order of their importance.

Cultural Factors : Three major cultural factors, *viz.*, religion, caste and value of children have been examined here. The percentage of adopters is significantly (at 1 per cent level) more among the Hindus than Muslims and Christians, irrespective of the number of children they currently have. Thus, the religion-wise variations in acceptance of family planning have been established. The lower percentage of contraception noticed among the Christians may be due to their lower socio-economic status among all the slum population. However, in this study it is confirmed that the adoption of contraception is directly related to the caste hierarchy. However, the hypothesis that those respondents who expressed greater preference on overall value of children (sons) may be less likely to adopt one or the other method of family planning as compared to those who mentioned moderate and low preference for value of children (sons), has also been supported with the data of the present study. No doubt on the basis of the three indicators of value of sons discussed here, it may be concluded that value of sons acts as one of the major barriers resulting in non-acceptance of contraception among the non-adopters.

Socio-economic Status : The type of house, educational status and occupational status of the respondents and their husbands and annual family income have been considered here as the socio-economic status variables in this study. In general, most status variables showed a negative relationship with acceptance of contraception, which is unexpected in respect of adoption and non-adoption of contraception. In other words, however, economic variables showed certain inconsistent relationship. Generally, it can be seen that the percentage of adopters is significantly higher (i) among the illiterates rather than those educated upto secondary or higher secondary level and (ii) among those respondents whose husbands are unskilled workers rather than those whose husbands are skilled and educated employees. These type of relationships may be due to the general poor socio-economic status conditions prevailing among the slum population. However, the annual family income of the respondents showed a somewhat positive association with a dip at the top.

Modernization and Status of Women : In the present study the following dimensions of modernization have been considered to measure the modernity level of the respondents, *viz.*, religious tolerance (secularism), views on higher age at marriage (18 + years) for girls, belief in fortune telling, type of medical treatment preferred for children and listening to mass media. The general level of modernization on most of these dimensions mentioned above is at a very low level among these slum dwellers even though they live in a metropolitan city like Madras. Consequently modernization in general could not make any definite influence on contraceptive behaviour. Hence more efforts need to be made to improve modern ideas, attitudes and knowledge among them through non-formal education.

In the present study an attempt is also made to measure the status of women in relation to the autonomy in decision-making by women and its influence on their contraceptive behaviour. The finding of the present study exhibited a somewhat positive curvelinear relationship between the index of female autonomy and adoption of family planning. On the other hand, a definite negative association between the roles of women (index) and adoption of contraception has been established. It may be because most of the slum women follow only traditional roles in their day to day life. Therefore, for emancipating the slum women concerted efforts may have to be made. Appropriate interventions based on scientific data may be promoted among them to diversify their roles to improve their status, which may in turn reduce morbidity, mortality and may ultimately reduce fertility.

Programme Factors : The programme variables considered in this study are : places of last delivery, persons who attended to last delivery, type of health centres visited, type of service rendered at such centres, availability of service in acceptable form, proximity of the service centres, satisfaction of service facilities (index), opinions and knowledge on incentives and whether incentives were received or not. The hypothesis considered here is that the percentage of acceptance of family planning will be higher among these respondents (i) whose place of delivery was hospitals rather than home ; (ii) whose deliveries were conducted by doctors or ANMs rather than untrained dai ; (iii) who utilized the services during pregnancy from the private and government hospitals rather than from traditional dais ; (iv) who felt that the services are available in an acceptable way and who got incentives for accepting contraception. The data supported the present hypothesis either at significant level or at least a trend was noticed.

Interestingly, it is fascinating to observe that the differentials in contraceptive acceptance and non-acceptance are statistically highly significant (X^2 = 213.962 ; Sig. at .01 level) when the respondents got satisfaction with the family planning service facilities (index). The regression findings also fully supported it and this factor alone explained 35 per cent of total variations in acceptance of contraception. Surprisingly the distance from the house of the respondents to the nearest sub-centre, PHC or hospital etc., and acceptance of contraception showed a negative association. This may be because of the well developed transport system in the slum area of Madras city and also due to the fact that OTC programmes are often arranged in distant places from the respondents' houses. Further, they may go to far off places to accept sterilization to keep the anonymity in order to avoid shyness or embarrassment.

Communication : Communication variables also played a big role in influencing the contraceptive behaviour. The percentage of adopters of contraception considerably increased among those respondents (i) who received family planning information from one or the other interpersonal sources of communication ; (ii) who reported that they mostly believe the advice given by the family planning workers and neighbours/relatives rather than others (Sig. at .01 level) ; (iii) who reported that radio is the best source of mass media for discriminating message on family planning (Sig. at .01 level) ; (iv) who attended the orientation camps on family planning (Sig. at .01 level) ; and (v) who heard of many success stories on family planning (Sig. at .01 level).

Interestingly, as expected, the differentials in contraceptive acceptance increased at a very high level as a result of respondents' discussion with satisfied adopters (X^2 = 52.5610 ; Sig. at .01 level). Thus, satisfied adopters have played a crucial role in influencing the respondents towards the adoption of family planning, which has also been confirmed through regression analysis.

Surprisingly the data of the present study confirmed that the percentage of adoption is significantly higher among those respondents who have not discussed with their husbands as against those who discussed (X^2 = 12.235 ; Sig. at 0.1 level) with their spouses. Adoption is greater among respondents who received message only once from workers rather than more than once and on several occasions (X^2 = 6.629 ; Sig. at .01 level). Thus, the latter hypothesis has been negatively proved. This may be because of the following reasons : (i) intensive motivation during the orientation camps ; and (ii) motivation during the post-natal period which is an appropriate occasion to get the best out of the extension educational efforts.

Demographic Variables : Age at marriage, present age of the respondents, duration of marriage, sex combination of the living children and duration of breastfeeding are the demographic factors taken into consideration here. Except the age at marriage, all the other variables have shown considerable positive influence on the adoption of family planning and thus the data supported fully the expected hypothesis in this regard. Further, number of living sons has turned out to be the second most important variable for the differentials in contraceptive behaviour which in fact is a cultural variable. The same has been confirmed through regression analysis also. There is definite sex preference among couples. The critical level of son preference is around 2 or 3 sons.

Surprisingly, age at marriage of the respondents (women) has exhibited an inconsistent but a somewhat negative relationship with the adoption of contraception. This may be because more young women who married early have adopted contraception.

Regression Findings

In the foregoing analysis we have seen the relationship between all the independent variables and contraceptive behaviour. But the extent of their influence in its totality on contraception, and also individual influence of variables could not be fully explored in the earlier chapters and hence some of the major variables are analysed through step-wise multiple linear regression analysis. For this purpose, 14 variables have been selected on the basis of their distinct influence on contraceptive behaviour (as seen from preceding analysis), theoretical importance, and also based on their characteristics. The results of this analysis are provided in Table 10.1.

Table 10.1 : Percentage of Total Sum of Squares Reduced for Contraceptive Behaviour in Step-wise Multiple Linear Regression Analysis

Variables	*Variations explained (in percentage)*
Total per cent of variations explained by all the selected variables	45.35
Level of satisfaction with service facilities (index)	34.98
Number of living sons (value of children)	4.39
Discussion with satisfied adopters	2.83
Religion	2.15

Note : Variables which have explained less than 2 per cent of the total contribution have been deleted.

According to Table 10.1, the total percentage of variation explained by all the major selected factors, *viz.*, respondents' level of satisfaction with service facilities (index), number of living sons (value of children), discussion with the satisfied adopters, and religion, together have contributed around 45.34 per cent of the total variations to explain the contraceptive behaviour.

Level of Satisfaction with Service Facilities : According to the regression analysis, respondents level of satisfaction with service facilities (index) is the single major variable, which has explained most of the variations in contraceptive behaviour. The percentage of variation explained by this variable alone is 34.98. How this variable was quantified as an index and its influence on contraception measured have been discussed in methodology chapter. *Thus, more than anything else, service facilities should be strengthened in an acceptable manner to induce non-adopters to accept contraception.* Hence, more action research also may have to be commissioned soon to develop a suitable and effective service delivery system for successfully promoting family planning programme.

The other three factors that explained the contraceptive behaviour through regression analysis are : value of children (number of sons), influence of satisfied adopters, and religious background of the couple. They together explained about 9.37 per cent of the variations in contraceptive behaviour. However, out of these factors the former (value of children) one is more important than the other two factors. In fact service-satisfaction, value of children and influence of satisfied adopters have already been confirmed as major determinants of contraceptive behaviour throughout the proceding tabulations. Here, once again they have shown their precise and exact level of influence in family planning. Thus, it can be concluded that creation of acceptable and effective service delivery system in family planning programme, followed by reassuring the survival chances of at least one son (value of children), involvement of effective change agents like satisfied adopters and suitable mass media, and parallel development of modern attitudes and status particularly among women, together may contribute to early and large scale adoption of contraception among slum population like the one discussed in this study.

The factors emerged as important through preceding tabulations and regression analysis together explain a major part of the determinants of contraceptive behaviour. Certain factors emerged as common in the analysis. However, certain variables could not show their importance in regression analysis because of the qualitative nature of the factors considered. Therefore, a combined consideration of all the preceding factors may together explain the salient determinants of contraceptive behaviour of the slum population studied here. It may be relevant for understanding contraceptive behaviour in similar population elsewhere in India too.

Implications

A number of programme oriented implications can be drawn out of the preceding findings. A few major recommendations are given below and many others can be gleaned out of the earlier discussions :

1. The findings of this study suggest that the respondents' satisfaction with the service facilities (index) has played a substantial role in the use of contraceptives. Hence, there is urgent need to provide proper health and family welfare services. Services on contraception should reach the doorsteps of the eligible couples. These arrangements may satisfy them, which in turn may increase the family planning adoption on a continued basis as noticed in this study.
2. Satisfied adopters may be used as convassers and motivators to disseminate family planning information, as well as to

motivate the eligible couples in general, which may create a favourabe attitude and carry more conviction.

3. Since religious background of the respondents is also playing a negative role in influencing contraceptive behaviour, all the religious leaders, especially priests in the churches and religious heads in the mosques may be encouraged to disseminate message on family planning.
4. Since value of children individually has a very great say in determining the use of contraception, the eligible couples in general, and the younger couples in particular, may have to be educated the need for giving equal preference for son and daughter. Further, those couples who are accepting use of permanent methods with only one daughter or two daughters without son, may be provided additional incentives in terms of cash or in terms of employment, life insurance policy etc. Of course, the Government of Maharashtra has already initiated a programme in this direction, which may be adopted in other places as well. According to the Maharashtra innovative scheme a couple will be provided with a life insurance policy worth Rs. 10,000/- and Rs. 5,000/- when they adopt contraception after having only one daughter and two daughters, respectively.
5. Since the level of modernisation and status of both of which are powerful and favourable factors for contraception, are low, special programmes may be promoted among slum dwellers to emancipate their women in general. These are only a few high priority implications for the promotion of family planning, and many more specific recommendations can be considered on the basis of the details of the preceding findings of this study.

BIBLIOGRAPHY

Abdullah et al., 1986 : "Family Planning in Jordon", Studies in Family Planning, 17(4), 200-203.

Agarwala, S.N. 1961 : Family Planning in Four Delhi Villages, Population Studies, 15(2), November, pp. 110-120.

Aiyappan, A. and Mahadevan, K. 1988 : Population and Social Change in an Indian Village, New Delhi, Mittal Publications.

Arnold, Fred et al., 1975 : The Value of Children — A Cross National Study, Hawaii, East-West Population Institute.

Arora, G. 1983 : "Socio-economic Determinants of Fertility". Journal of Family Welfare 29(3) : 39.

Arora, S. 1966 : Study of Diffusion Process. Unpublished Dissertation of Masters Degree of Nursing. New Delhi, Delhi University.

ASI Market Research Inc., 1974 : A follow-up study of the Effectiveness of Family Planning Communications in the Republic of Korea. Seoul : pp. 1-60.

Audinarayana, N. 1981 : Socio-economic Determinants of Age at Marriage. Unpublished M. Phil. thesis, Tirupati, Dept. of Population Studies, S.V. University, (Mimeo).

———————. 1986 : "The Influence of Age at Marriage on Fertility and Fertility Behaviour". The Journal of Family Welfare, 33(1), pp. 56-62.

———————. 1987 : "Determinants of Family Planning Acceptance in India", The Journal of Family Welfare, 33(4), pp. 64-69.

Barbara et al., 1981 : "Contraceptive Use and Fertility in Honduras 1981-1984". Studies in Family Planning 8(5) : 296-299, September.

Bhate, Vaijayanti, 1984 : "Family Planning Behaviour in Maharashtra", Paper presented at the National Seminar on Ten Years of Family Planning Evaluation Studies in India, Bombay, IIPS, (March, 20-22).

Bhatia, J.C. 1983 : "Age at Marriage and Fertility in Chana (West Africa)". Demography India : 12(2) : 185.

Bhatia, J.C. 1979 : "Status of Women and Fertility in India". Journal of Family Welfare. 25(3) : 20.

Bhatia, Sushan, 1982 : "Contraceptive Insertions and Subsequent Behaviour in Rural Bangladesh. Studies in Family Planning 13(1) : 24-29.

Bhargava, Y. 1968 : An Evaluation of a few of the Family Planning Posters. Unpublished dissertation, Delhi, University of Delhi, Lady Irwin College.

Bhende, A. 1968 : Impact of Radio Broadcast on IUCD in Five Years of Research in Family Planning. Bomaby : IIPS, (Miemo), 43-44.

Bhuyan, S.B. & Bhuyan, K.C. 1984 : "Nuptiality, Fertility and Family Planning Practices in Rural Bangladesh, A Case Study", Journal of Family Welfare, 31(1) : 62.

Blake, J. 1965 : "Demographic Science and the Redirection of Population Policy", in Public Health and Population Change (Eds.) by M.C. Sheps and J.C. Ridley, Pittsburgh : University of Pittsburgh Press, 41-69.

Caldwell, J.C. 1967 : Fertility Attitude in three economically contrasting rural regions of Ghana. Economic Development and Cultural Change, 15 : 217-38.

——————————. 1968 : The Control of Family Size in Tropical Africa. Demography, 5(2) : 598-619.

Ca. ıpbell, A. 1968 : The Role of Family Planning in the Reduction of Poverty. Journal of Marriage and the Family, 30 : 236-45.

Carvajal, M.J. & Gaithman, David, T. 1976 : Family Planning and Family Size Determination : The Evidence from Seven Latin American Cities. Gainesville : The University Press of Florida.

Chandra, Shanta Kohli, 1987 : Family Planning Programme in India. Foreword by T.N. Chaturvedi, New Delhi : Mital Publications.

Chandrasekaran, C. & Kuder, K. 1965 : Family Planning Through Clinics. Bombay : Allied Publishers Private Ltd.

Chandrasekaran, C. & Bebarta, P.C. 1963 : The relative role of information sources in the dissemination of knowledge of family planning methods in Bombay city. Journal of Family Welfare, 9(94) : 5-14.

Danda, K. 1984 : Family Planning : An Adoptive Strategy, New Delhi : Inter India Publications.

Dorthy Nortman & Jones Gravin, 1968 : Roman Catholic Fertility and Family Planning. Studies in Family Planning, 34(3) ; October.

Dubey, D.C. 1967 : Adoption of a New Contraceptive in Urban India. Monograph No. 7, New Delhi : Central Family Planning Institute.

Dubey, D.C. & Goldein, M.M 1967 : Communication and Diffusion of the IUCD : A Case study in Urban India. Demography, 4(2), pp. 601-14

Fatima, Nikhat, 1977 : "Attitude of Muslim Women of Aligarh Muslim University to Family Planning", Journal of Family Welfare, 24(1), 23.

Fisek, N.H. et al., 1968 : Fertility Control in Turkey. Demography 5(2) ; 578-89.

Ford Foundation, Lagos, 1972 : Family Planning of Nigeria, Personal Communication to W.O. Sweeney, p. 16.

Freedman, R. 1959 : "Social Values about family size in the U.S.". In Population Conference, Vienna, 1959. Vienna : IUSSP, pp. 173-83.

____________________ . 1963 : "Norms for Family size in under developed areas " in Proceedings of the Royal Society, B. 139 (974) 220-40, London : Royal Society.

____________________ . 1968 : "Norms for Family size in under developed areas" in Population and Society (Ed.) by Charles, B. Nam, pp.. 215-30.

Ghosal, A.K. & Sarkar, B.N. 1987 : "Prospect of Family Planning in Fertility Decline in Rural West Bengal", Population, Family and Culture (Eds.) R.N. Pati, New Delhi, Ashish Publishing House, pp. 2-20.

Government of India, 1986 : "Evaluation Report on Family Planning Programme", Programme Evaluation Organization, Planning Commission, New Delhi : Government of India, 10-23 (May 1984).

____________________ . 1988 : Family Welfare Programme in India, Year Book 1987-88, New Delhi, Department of Ministry of Health and Family Welfare.

Goyal, R.P. 1965 : A Survey of Fertility and Family Planning in Western Uttar Pradesh, Delhi, Institute of Economic Growth (Mimeo).

Goode William, J. 1963 : World Revolution and Family Patterns. Glencoe III : Free Press, p. 230.

Heer, David, M. 1964 : Fertility Differences between Indian and Spanish speaking parts of Andean Countries. Population Studies, 17 : (1), 71-84.

Hein, Catherine, R. 1977: "Family Planning in Mauritus: A National Survey", Studies in Family Planning, 8(12) : 316-319 (December).

Hill, et al., 1959 : The Family and Population Control : A Puerto-Rican Experiment in Social Change. Chapel Hill, N.C. The University of North Carolina Press.

Indian Institute of Public Opinion (IIPO). 1964. "A Survey of Awareness and Practice of Family Planning". Monthly Public Opinion Survey, 9(6 & 7), (March and April).

____________________. 1967 : Urban Attitudes Towards Family Planning : A Survey in Eleven Cities, Monthly Public Opinion Survey, 13(1).

Jacob, Paul. 1965 : "Report on a Study of the General Attitude Towards Family Planning in Hooghly District", Public Preferences Survey, West Bengal 1962-63, Calcutta, Technical Note No. 32, Indian Statistical Institute.

Jha et al., 1969 : Family Planning Attitudes and Practices in Women : A Study of Two Groups. The Journal of Family Welfare, 16(1), 10-24.

Johnson, G.Z. 1960 : "Differential Fertility in European Countries", in Demographic and Economic Change in Developed Countries. Princeton, National Bureau of Economic Research. Princeton University Press, pp. 36-72.

Kanitkar Tara & Murthy. B.N. 1983 : "Factors Associated with Contraception in Bihar and Rajasthan", Dynamics of Population and Family Welfare (Eds) K.S. Srinivasan and S., Mukherji, Bombay, Himalaya Publishing House, pp. 179-186.

Karlin, B. & Ali, S.M. 1968 : The use of the radio in support of the family planning programme in Hyderabad district of West Pakistan. Pakistan Journal of Family Planning. 2(2) : 1-31, July.

Kapil, K.K. 1967 : Promotion of Inter-spouse communication in Family Planning as a result of educational sessions in the Post-natal clinics. Bombay, Newsletter, 32, IIPS.

Kaur, Malkit, Sharma, M.L. & Kaur Satram, 1988 : "Health and Family Planning Services among Rural Women in Haryana", Kurukshetra, Vol. 36(11), 11-14 and 17.

Kaur, Surjit, 1974 : Family Planning in Two Industrial Units, New Delhi : Council for Social Development.

Khan, M.E. 1979 : Family Planning among Muslims in India. New Delhi : Manchar Publication.

Kirk, Dudley, 1966 : "Factors affecting Muslims Natality, in Family Planning and Planned birth programmes (Eds). Bernard Berelson, et al., Chicago : University of Chicago Press, pp. 561-79.

Kiser, C.V. et al., 1968 : Trends and Variations in Fertility in the United States. Cambridge, Mass : Harvard University Press.

Knodel John & Prachuabinsh, Vist. 1976 : Preference for sex of children in Thailand : A Comparison of Husbands and wives' attitude., Studies in Family Planning. 7(5), 137-48.

Knodel, et al., 1984 : "Infant feeding practice, Post-partum Amenorrhea and Contraceptive use in Thailand", Studies in Family Planning, 161(1) : 302-311.

Korean Institute of Family Planning (KIFP), 1979 : The 1976 National Fertility and Family Planning Survey, KIFP, pp. 153-190.

Kwon et al., 1970 : "A Study on urban population control : Song dong Go Action Research Project on Family Planning and Fertility", in Population and Family Planning in the Republic of Korea, Vol. 1, Seoul : Ministry of Health and Social Affairs, pp. 550.

Lieu, R. et al., 1970 : The Ceber Family Health Project. Centre for the Study of Man in Contemporary Society. Indiana : University of Notre Dame.

Mahadevan, K. 1979 : Sociology of Fertility. New Delhi, Sterling Publications.

—————————. 1984 : Decision-making and Diffusion in Family Planning, Tirupati, S.V. University.

—————————. 1984 ; Strategies for Population Control, Tiruptai : S.V. University.

—————————. 1985 : Infant and Childhood Mortality in India. New Delhi, Mittal Publications.

—————————. 1986 : Fertility and Mortality : Theory, Methodology and Empirical Issues, New Delhi, Sage Publications.

—————————. 1989 : Fertility Policies of Asian Countries, New Delhi, Sage Publications.

—————————. 1989 : Population Dynamics of Indian States. New Delhi, Mittal Publications.

—————————. 1989 : Women, Society and Population Dynamics of Asian Countries, New Delhi, Sage Publications.

Mahadevan, K. & Sumangala, 1987 : Social Development, Cultural Change and Fertility Decline : A Study of Fertility Change in Kerala. New Delhi, Sage Publications.

Mamdani, Mahmood, 1972 : The Myth of Population Control : Family Caste and Class in an Indian Village, New York : Monthly Review Press.

Michael, Andreu, 1967 : Interaction and Family Planning in French Urban Families. Demography, 4(2) : 615-525.

Morrison, William, A. 1956 : Attitudes of males towards family planning in a western Indian village. Milbank Memorial Fund Quarterly, 34(2), 274-81, July.

Mukherjee, R. 1976 : Family Planning in India. Madras : Orient Longmans.

Mukherjee, B.N. 1975 : The role of husband-wife communication in family planning. Journal of Marriage and Family, 37(3) : 655-67.

__________________ . 1975 : Marital decision-making and family planning. The Journal of Family Planning 21(3).

Muleitha and Kaur, B. 1962 : "Family Planning investigation in urban and rural population", All India Institute of Hpgeine and Public Health, Calcutta, Alumni Association Bulletin, 11, 21.

Nayar, P.S.G. & George, N.V. 1972 : Correlates of inter district variations in the process of family planning in Kerala. The Journal of Family Welfare, 18(3), 46.

Notestein, et al., 1968 : The Population Dilemma, Bombay : Jaico Publication House.

Oni, A. Gbolahan & James McCarthey, 1986 : Use of Contraceptives for Birth Spacing in Nigerian city". Studies in Family Planning, 11(2) : 377-379 (December, 1980).

Operations Research Group, 1972 : Family Planning Practices in India, Baroda.

Park, H.J. 1967 : "Use and relative effectiveness of various channels of communications in the development of the Korean Family Planning Programme", Report of the working group on communication aspects of family planning programmes and selected papers. Bangkok : U.N. ECAFE.

Patel, V.M. 1968 : A Study of the effectiveness of radio as a medium of communication. The Journal of Family Welfare, 14, (3), 57-62.

Pillai, K.M. 1971, Study of Decision process in adopting family planning methods. Gandhigram : Bulletin of the Gandhigram Institute of Rural Health and Family Planning (1), 6 : 41-56.

Poffenberger, Thomas & Poffenberger, S.B. 1968 : Motivational aspects of resistance to family planning in an Indian village. Demography 5(2) : 757-66.

—————————. 1969 : Husband-wife communication in an Indian village. New Delhi : Central Family Planning Institute, IX, 108.

—————————. 1972 : "The social psychology of fertility behaviour in a village in India". James T. Fawcett (Eds.) — Psychological Perspectives and Population. New York : Basic Books, pp. 135-62.

Population Problems Research Council. The Mainichi Newspapers. 1970—Family Planning in Japan : Opinion Survey by the Mainichi Newspapers. Tokyo : Japanese Organisation for International Co-operation in Family Planning, pp. 239.

Population Services International, 1976 : (Preethi Campaign), Draft Prepared for Publications, Spring, 1976, 33.

Presser, H.B. & L.L. Bumpass, 1970 : The acceptability of Contraceptive Sterilization among United States Couples : 1970. Family Planning Perspectives, Vol. 44(1). 18-26.

Rajaretnam, T.C. 1986 : "The Relationship between age at Marriage and Fertility : Some evidence from a rural area in Tamil Nadu". GIRH & FW Bulletin, Vol. 21, No. 3, 1986 December, pp. 31-55.

Rahman et al., 1980 : Contraceptive Distribution in Bangladesh". Some Lessons learned. Studies in Family Planning, 11(6) : 191-201.

Rainwater, L. 1965 : Family design : Marital sexuality, family size and contraception. Chicago : Chicago Aldine, 349.

Rao, N.B. & Kulkarni, P.M. & P.H. Rayappa, 1985 : Determinants of Fertility Decline : A Study of Rural Karnataka. New Delhi, South Asian Publishers.

Rele, J.R. and Tara Kanitkar, 1980 : Fertility and Family Planning in Greater Bombay : Bombay - Popular Prakashan.

Ridley et al., 1969 : On the apparent sub-fecundity of non-family planners. Social Biology 16 : 24-28 (March).

Robert, B.J. et al., 1965 : Family Planning Survey in Dacca. East Pakistan. Demography 2(1), 74-96.

Reddy, V.M. 1984 : The Influence of Demographic Variables on the Adoption of Sterilization. The Journal of Family Welfare, 30(3).

Reddy, M.M. 1985 : Sex combination of Living Children and the Adoption of Sterilization. The Journal of Family Welfare, Vol. 31(4), (June).

Reddy, P.J. 1984 : A Study on practice of contraceptives in

Hyderabad city. Paper presented at the National Seminar on Ten Years of Family Planning Evaluation Studies in India, Bombay : IIPS.

Sahawney, Y.L. & Langoo, P.N. 1959 : A Study of male sterilization in Jammu and Kashmir. Family Planning News 2(2).

Sarma, D.V.N. & Jain, A.K. 1974 : Preference about sex of children and use of contraception among women wanting no more children in India. Demography India, 3(1) : 81-104.

Sarupriya, Shanti, L 1964 : Attitude towards family planning in a small urban community. Indian Journal of Social Work, 25(1) : 79-87.

Sathar Zeba, A. & Chidambaram, V.C. 1984 : Differentials in Contraceptive use. Voorburg, Netherlands : WFS Comparative Studies No. 36. International Statistical Institute.

Sengupta, A. & Roy, S. Guha 1969 : Discovering the Degree of commitment of family planning in a Calcutta city project. Calcutta : Family Planning Research Unit, Technical Paper No. 29, ISI (Mimeo).

Shaktawat, 1974 : Adoption behaviour towards family planning — A diagnostic analysis. The Journal of Family Welfare 21(2).

Shakilarani, R. 1989 ; Contraceptive Behaviour and its Determinants in a Tamil Nadu Village. Unpublished M. Phil. Dissertation, Coimbatore : Department of Population Studies, Bharatiar University.

Siddha, K.K. 1974 : Family Planning : The Religious Factor. New Delhi : Abhinav Publishing.

Siddique, M.K.A. 1965 : Attitude towards family planning in the Slums of Calcutta. Population Review, 9(1), 86-91.

Siva Raju, S. 1982 : Factors Influencing region-wise differential performing in family planning achievement. Unpublished Ph.D. thesis. Department of Population Studies, S.V. University. Tirupati.

—————————. 1987 : "Socio-economic Factors in Family Planning Adoption", Social Change 17(1) : 54-56, (March).

Singh, J.P. & Gupta, A. 1983 : Social Consideration of Sterilization. Demography India, Vol. 12(1), 74-85.

Soeradji Budi & Sri Harijati Hatmodji, 1981 : Contraceptive use in Java-Bali : A Multivariate analysis on the determinants of contraceptive use. Asian Population Studies Series No. 49, Multivariate analysis of World Fertility Survey data for selected

ESCAP countries. Report and selected papers of the Regional Workshop and Seminar (ST/ESCAP/151), pp. 68-85.

Som, R.K. and Sengupta, S. 1960 : Survey of Opinion on Optimum Number of Children and attitude towards family planning, West Bengal, New Delhi, Studies in Family Planning, Directorate General of Health Services, Government of India, 45-53.

Srinivasan, K. & Kachirayan, M. 1968 : Vasectomy follow-up study : Findings and Implications. Bulletin of the Gandhigram Institute of Rural Health and Family Welfare, 31(1) - 30-31.

Srivastava, J.N. 1974 : A Study of inter-district variations in family planning acceptance in Uttar Pradesh, Series-C, Occasional paper No. 8, Lucknow, DRC, Dept. of Economics, Lucknow University.

Srivastava, G.P.L. 1975 : Inter-block variations in family planning achievements. The Journal of Family Welfare, 20(4), 34-42.

Stycos, J.M. 1970 : Education and Fertility in Pureto Rico", Social Demography (Ed.) Thomas R. Ford and Gordon, P. De Jong, pp. 454-455.

Sung, Kyu-Taik, 1977 : Patient's evaluation of family planning services ; the case of inter-city clinics. Studies in Family Planning 8(5) : 130-37.

Swee-Hock, Saw, G.S. et al., 1958 : Family Planning, KAP in Malaya : Demography, 5(2) ; 702-709.

Sweeney, W.O. 1977 : Media Communications in Population/Family Planning Programmes : A Reivew : Population Reports, J.(16) : Baltimore, John Hopkins University (294-303).

Thangadorai, M. 1987. Communication in Family Planning Adoption. Unpublished Ph.D. Thesis, Tirupati, Dept. of Population Studies, S.V. University.

Tsui et al., 1981 : Contraceptive Availability, Differentials in use and Fertility. Studies in Family Planning, 12(11) : 386-391 (November).

United Nations, 1961 : Mysore Population Study (ST/SOA/SER/A/34), New York.

—————————. 1975 : Husband-wife Communication and the practice of family planning. Asian Population Studies Series No. 17, Bangkok : ESCAP.

Vasa, Sumti, 1967 : IUCD and its different aspects : A Study of 400 cases. Family Planning News 8(10) : 7-12.

Walvekar, Vandana et al., 1974 : Social Aspects of Family Planning : A Study of 600 cases. The Journal of Family Welfare, 20(4) : 21-24.

Weller, H. Robert, 1968 : The employment of wives, dominance, and fertility. Journal of Marriage and the family 39(2), 437-42. (August).

Whelpton, P.K. et al., 1966 : Fertility and Family Planning in the United States. New Jersey. Princeton : Princeton University Press.

Wyon, John B. & John E. Gordon, 1971 : The Khanna Study : Population Problems in the Rural Punjab, Cambridge : Harvard University Press.

Zachariah, K.C. 1983 : Anomaly of Fertility Decline in Kerala. Report No. LPRO 671-70, Washington : World Bank.

INDEX